Lyrics for Life

Lyrics for Life
Selected Psalms

This inductive Bible study is designed for individual, small group, or classroom use. A leader's guide with full lesson plans and the answers to the Bible study questions is available from Regular Baptist Press. Order RBP1709 online at www.RegularBaptistPress.org, e-mail orders@rbpstore.org, call toll-free 1-800-727-4440, or contact your distributor.

REGULAR BAPTIST PRESS
1300 North Meacham Road
Schaumburg, Illinois 60173-4806

The Doctrinal Basis of Our Curriculum

A more detailed statement with references is available upon request.

- The verbal, plenary inspiration of the Scriptures
- Only one true God
- The Trinity of the Godhead
- The Holy Spirit and His ministry
- The personality of Satan
- The Genesis account of creation
- Original sin and the fall of man
- The virgin birth of Christ
- Salvation through faith in the shed blood of Christ
- The bodily resurrection and priesthood of Christ
- Grace and the new birth
- Justification by faith
- Sanctification of the believer
- The security of the believer
- The church
- The ordinances of the local church: baptism by immersion and the Lord's Supper
- Biblical separation— ecclesiastical and personal
- Obedience to civil government
- The place of Israel
- The pretribulation rapture of the church
- The premillennial return of Christ
- The millennial reign of Christ
- Eternal glory in Heaven for the righteous
- Eternal torment in Hell for the wicked

LYRICS FOR LIFE: SELECTED PSALMS
Adult Bible Study Book
Vol. 56, No. 2
© 2007
Regular Baptist Press • Schaumburg, Illinois
www.RegularBaptistPress.org • 1-800-727-4440
Printed in U.S.A.
RBP1712 • ISBN: 978-1-59402-480-1

Contents

Preface

Though written over a 1,000-year period and compiled around 2,500 years ago, the book of Psalms is one of the most often visited books of the Bible. Written as poetic songs, the psalms are timeless in their appeal and valuable in their revelation of God and life. We can go to the book of Psalms and find encouragement and strength as well as instruction and challenge. Through them we can fathom the depths of God and learn to respond to Him in praise.

This course will present God's songs on subjects such as true happiness, God's provision, confession of sin, and singing to the Lord. As you work your way through this course, you will find that the psalms are truly Lyrics for Life.

The Way of Happiness

Responding to situations according to God's Word brings happiness.

Psalm 1

"Blessed is the man that walketh not in the counsel of the ungodly, nor standeth in the way of sinners, nor sitteth in the seat of the scornful. But his delight is in the law of the LORD; and in his law doth he meditate day and night" (Psalm 1:1, 2).

Every day we come into contact with various influences, and they shape our lives. People influence us. Our spouses and friends influence us. Financial considerations influence us. The media influence us. Advertising is such an important part of our culture that some people allow companies to put advertising on their cars and even on their bodies! One young man promised to wear any company's ad-bearing T-shirt every day for six months if the company would pay him $1,500. Another young man made his arm available for any company's ad in the form of a tattoo if the company would pay him $5,000. Someone else made his back available for a tattoo for $7,000, while a car owner offered his car as a rolling billboard to any company that would give him $8,000. Influences will never go away. So, to be successful Christians, we must determine which influences to accept and which to avoid.

Getting Started

1. What are some subtle influences on your life?

2. Why is it important to recognize what influences you?

Psalm 1 helps us understand which influences we should avoid and which ones we should allow to mold us.

Searching the Scriptures

Psalm 1 is an appropriate introduction for the book of the Psalms, for it summarizes the two ways, or courses, a person may choose: the way of the ungodly or the way of the godly. Consequently, this psalm can be classified as a wisdom psalm. It has remarkable similarity to the book of Proverbs and its description of the two ways a person may choose.

The first word in Psalm 1, "blessed," sets the tone for the entire psalm. The word literally means "happy." So we have here a divine prescription for true happiness.

3. How would you define true happiness?

True happiness is not merely a good feeling; it is an inward, deep-seated contentment and satisfaction in the life God has given to a believer, no matter what the circumstances.

4. The psalmist used a plural form of the word "happy," which could be translated, "O the happinesses of the man" or "How completely happy is the man." What do you think the psalmist was trying to convey in doing so?

What to Avoid

Blessed, or happy, individuals are first characterized by what they do not do—they do not allow unbelievers to influence them. Using poetic parallelism, the psalmist portrayed this concept in three statements, each showing a different level of influence.

5. Study verse 1 and complete the chart below, indicating the action involved, what to avoid, and the name for the ungodly.

Action	What to Avoid	Name for the Ungodly
1.		
2.		
3.		

6. What increasing levels of influence do you see in the words "walking," "standing," and "sitting"?

"Walking" indicates a casual influence from the ungodly, similar to a person's walking and talking with someone in a relaxed atmosphere. This influence can be deceiving, since it may seem harmless. However, it can lead to listening to the advice of the ungodly or observing their waywardness and actively considering them. Watching television, particularly programs that encourage sinful lifestyles, is a subtle means of influence that believers often consider harmless. "I'm not living that way," we might claim. But when we watch others sin, we can't help but be influenced by them. Choosing to watch sin in action is to choose to walk in the counsel of the ungodly.

"Standing" involves more than simply walking and conversing casually; it portrays a person who has stopped to have a serious conversation with the unrighteous. The word conveys a fixed association and an actual identification with the sinner's way of life. Choosing unbelieving close friends who are actively living in sin is a primary means of standing in the same path with sinners. Having unbelieving friends is not wrong, but when we allow them to set the tone for our lives, we are headed for trouble. For example, allowing them to swear, gossip, blaspheme God, and talk in a crude manner around us as if we approve their behavior is to stand in the same path with sinners. Those who stand with sinners are hiding their lights and trying to blend in with a sinful society (Matthew 5:13–16). This is a dangerous way to live. The unchecked, sinful influence of close friends can eventually drag a believer into sin.

"Sitting" with the scorner is the strongest level of influence. It means a believer has become so influenced by the person that the believer has taken up permanent dwelling and has established his or her residence with the scorner. The believer now acts like those who despise God's ways. Believers who are sitting with the scorner act and speak like an unbeliever.

7. Read the following passages: Genesis 13:7–13; 14:11, 12; 19:1, 12–26, 30–38. Lot, Abraham's nephew, allowed himself to be affected by an increasing level of ungodly influence. What were the tragic results?

8. What are some examples of each level of influence in our lives today?

Walking—

Standing—

Sitting—

Righteous people who desire true happiness do not take the first step of walking with the ungodly lest they end up sitting with them.

9. What steps should believers take to start backing away from the ungodly influences of unbelievers?

10. What can you do to be a godly influence in the life of an unbeliever without being negatively influenced by that person?

What a Delight!

In Psalm 1:2 the psalmist turned our attention to what a truly blessed, or happy, person does. This person is influenced, not by the ungodly, but by the Scriptures. The "law" is the familiar Hebrew word "torah." This "law" is not just the Ten Commandments or even the Pentateuch. Rather it is any instruction from the Lord, no matter where we find it. Though the psalmist had in mind the Old Testament writings available at that time, we understand this word to embody all of Scripture.

11. a. What does it mean to delight in the Scriptures?

b. What are some evidences of delighting in the Scriptures?

12. What image do Psalm 42:1 and 2 contain that helps us understand about delighting in God's Word?

Reading and studying the Scriptures is not a burden but a joy. We should look forward to our time in the Word each day.

13. What words describe the concept of meditation?

Some have compared meditating to a cow's chewing its cud, and that is probably a good analogy. That is the kind of action we are to take toward the law of God—mulling it over in our minds until we understand its full meaning.

14. What do the words "day and night" mean in relation to meditating on God's Word?

We often associate meditation with what we do in our daily devotional time. While our daily time with God is important, meditating on God's Word involves more than daily devotions. It involves something we should be doing "day and night." If we read and study our Bible in the morning, we are to think about it whenever we get an opportunity to.

15. According to Joshua 1:8, what is the purpose or goal of meditating on God's Word?

We are to remember and ruminate on the Word throughout the day and night so we can apply the wisdom of Scripture to the events of our days and nights. Knowing and meditating on God's Word has little value if we do not let it influence our lives.

Fruit

A believer who allows the law of God to influence him or her will be a spiritually fruitful person (Psalm 1:3). The psalmist illustrated this truth by comparing the believer to a tree.

16. Read Psalm 1:3. What four benefits come to the person who lets his or her life be influenced by the Word?

17. When have you seen the benefits of delighting in God's Word in your life or in the life of a friend?

Not So for the Ungodly

Verses 1–3 of Psalm 1 describe in detail the blessing and prosperity of the righteous, but the way of the wicked receives only a terse and abrupt treatment. This abruptness can be seen in the literal translation of verse 4: "Not so the wicked." It almost seems that that psalmist did not want to dwell on such an unpleasant subject.

He went on to compare the wicked to chaff. Chaff is debris—the husks and pieces of the grain plant separated from the seeds at harvest. A winnower would toss a mixture of chaff and grain into the air so the lighter chaff would blow away.

18. Why is chaff an appropriate analogy for unbelievers?

Using poetic parallelism again, the psalmist affirmed that the ungodly will not be able to stand before the judgment of God or have a standing in the assembly of righteous people. Unbelievers may think they are good enough to merit some favor from God, but they will soon learn that they cannot stand their ground. The ungodly will have to sit down or cower in shame and guilt. They will be alienated from the people of God.

19. Contrast the description of the unrighteous in Psalm 1:5 with the description of the righteous in Romans 8:1.

Psalm 1 concludes by contrasting again the godly and the ungodly. The Lord knows, or is intimately acquainted with, the righteous. "The Lord knoweth them that are his" (2 Timothy 2:19). But the ungodly will perish in Hell for eternity (John 3:18; 2 Peter 2:12; Revelation 20:13, 14).

20. Read Psalm 1:6. Why should knowing that God is intimately acquainted with us bring us happiness as nothing else can?

Making It Personal

If we are to be truly happy, we must respond to every situation in accordance with God's Word. We must first delight in and spend time in God's Word. Then we are to meditate on the Word day and night so we can relate Biblical truth to every situation or problem we face. Review Joshua 1:8 to get a clear picture of what God wants from us.

21. What problems or situations are you facing right now? Take time to write three of them below.

1.

2.

3.

What Biblical truths should influence you in your response to those situations? Beside the problems or situations above, write the Biblical responses you should make.

22. Write a commitment to God to respond Biblically to the problems you are currently facing.

23. Take time to memorize Psalm 1:1 and 2.

His Undeserved Attention

God graciously gives us His
undeserved attention.

Psalm 8

"O LORD our Lord, how excellent is thy name in all the earth! who hast set thy glory above the heavens" (Psalm 8:1).

Two blind beggars waited as Jesus came down the road. They asked Jesus to heal them, and He did (Matthew 9:27–31). Did they deserve such attention? No, they had done nothing to merit the touch of the Savior. At another time, Jesus met a funeral party making its way to the burial of a mother's only son (Luke 7:11–17). When Jesus touched the coffin, the son returned to life. Did the mother or son deserve such attention from the Savior? No, the mother and her son were the recipients of undeserved attention from the Lord. Frequently Jesus felt compassion for undeserving people and showed His attention to them by healing them.

Getting Started

1. Have you ever received something or been recognized for something you honestly did not deserve? How did you feel?

2. Has someone important, famous, or rich ever paid attention to you personally? How did you feel?

When someone important pays attention to us or we receive something we honestly did not deserve, we usually feel humbled, undeserving, and appreciative. Our Bible study in Psalm 8 will help us get a clear picture of the undeserved attention that God gives us and how we should respond.

Searching the Scriptures

Psalm 8 is a praise psalm. In this short piece, David marveled at God's majesty and glory and praised Him for His undeserved attention to us.

Praise the Lord!

3. Take time to read the psalm aloud several times. Note the frequent use of parallelism.

First, David addressed God by the name "LORD." This name (note the small capital letters in the word) is how Bible translators treat the Hebrew word pronounced Yahweh (or our anglicized version, Jehovah). This name is the personal name God gave for Himself to His people. It indicates His self-existence, His strength, and His commitment to the covenants He made with Israel.

The Israelites had such great reverence for the name "Jehovah" that they refused to pronounce it, substituting another name. While we are not prohibited from pronouncing God's name, we should maintain great reverence for this and all His names.

David then addressed God by the name "Lord." (Note the lowercase letters in the word, distinguishing this name from the first one.) This is the word from which we get the name "Adonai." This name refers to God as the sovereign, or master, and to His dominion over creation.

4. What did David convey about God in these two names?

David declared that God's name is excellent throughout all the earth. To say that His name is "excellent" means it is marked by majesty, splendor, and magnificence. God's name is more than a means of identification, as our names are for us. His name is the sum total of His attributes. His name expresses Who He is in all His fullness. Many today do not acknowledge God's name as excellent and majestic, but someday all will acknowledge it (Philippians 2:9–11). Praise the Lord for His excellent name!

5. What was David communicating by his description of God's glory in verse 1?

God's majesty and glory are everywhere—throughout the earth and above the heavens. Praise the Lord for His glorious name!

After his outburst of praise, David reflected in verses 2–8 on the reasons for such praise: the undeserved attention God gives to people. Throughout these verses David seemed to have all mankind—righteous and unrighteous—in mind. However, we believers look at these thoughts from the perspective of God's personal care for His own.

God Uses Children

6. What does verse 2 tell us about how God uses children?

Christ quoted Psalm 8:2 after He cleansed the temple for the second time (Matthew 21:12–16). The children in the temple witnessed Christ's healing of the blind and the lame and cried, "Hosanna to the son of David!" (v. 15). The children were in essence recognizing Jesus as the Messiah. Such an act angered the chief priests and scribes, who saw that Jesus was influencing the next generation. When the leaders questioned the validity of the children's praise (v. 16), Christ responded by quoting Psalm 8:2. The children's praise was right on target. God's Son is worthy of praise. That God used *children* to declare this worthiness is humbling.

David marveled that God uses the "strength" (puny as it is) of little children to silence His enemies (Psalm 8:2). How could a child defend the Lord against His enemies? Returning to the incident of the religious leaders criticizing the children for recognizing Jesus as the Messiah, we notice that the religious leaders, not the children, were silenced (Matthew 21:15, 16). There is no record of continued protest by the religious leaders. And the passage doesn't state that the children stopped their praising of Christ at the word of the religious leaders. We can surmise that the children continued to praise Christ as the religious leaders stood silent. The Lord used humble children to silence His enemies. What a privilege for the children in the temple that day!

7. What are some ways the words or actions of children might refute those who dishonor the Lord?

Sometimes God uses little children to soften the hearts of hardened parents and grandparents, leading to their salvation. God also uses children in science class in school to silence people by speaking the simple truth of creation.

8. In what way is God's use of children an instance of our undeserved attention from Him?

9. What do 1 Corinthians 1:25 and 27 add to the truth of Psalm 8:2?

God gives undeserved attention to children. He lets their words and actions defend Him. Praise the Lord for using little children!

Thinking of Us

David then turned his attention to another example of our undeserved attention from God: His attention to men and women in general. David scanned the vastness of God's creation in the night sky and marveled that God would give any attention to men and women (Psalm 8:3, 4). As David gazed into the sky, he observed the moon and the myriad distant stars.

10. Read Psalm 8:3. How did David describe the heavenly bodies?

As David reflected on the vastness of the universe (and he did not have any idea of its full extent), he marveled that God would give attention to puny, insignificant mankind. In typical Hebrew parallel style, he exclaimed in verse 4,
"What is man, that thou art mindful of him?
"And the son of man, that thou visitest him?"
What is man compared to the galaxies, stars, and other heavenly bodies? Why would God give any attention to mankind? Instead of being unaware of men and women, God knows all about them. Verse 4 uses the English word "mindful," which conveys the idea that God's mind is full of thoughts about us! Psalm 139:17 affirms this truth: "How precious also are thy thoughts unto me, O God! How great is the sum of them." Instead of visiting, or afflicting, people with judgment, God visits, or comforts, them with care and concern. This overwhelming thought led David to say, "O LORD our Lord, how excellent is thy name in all the earth!" (8:9).

11. Try to put God's interest in small mankind in perspective by completing the following comparison: God's being interested in mankind is like a person's being interested in . . . (e.g., every flee crawling around on the back of a cat or dog).

12. What are some ways God gives attention to men and women in general?

Praise the Lord for His being mindful of us!

Our Privileged Position

As David reflected on the fact that God cares for us at all, he was further impressed that God would actually give these small creatures called humans a dignified role in His order.

13. In verse 5 what did David say about mankind when he wrote that man is "a little lower than the angels"?

14. What does the theory of evolution do to the exalted position of mankind in God's creation?

David reinforced the truth of the first phrase in verse 5 by declaring that God has crowned mankind with glory and honor. David spoke about the glory of God in verse 1; then he declared that men (and by implication, women) also possess this characteristic (v. 5). The use of the word "crowned" points again to the dignity God has vested in mankind.

God further showed His undeserved attention to Adam's race by giving Adam and his progeny dominion over His creation and by putting all things under their feet (vv. 6–8). Mankind, with its regal position, is to rule over the animal kingdom. David enumerated the domesticated animals (sheep and oxen), wild animals, birds, and fish. He again showed his familiarity with the Creation account in Genesis 1 and God's command to exercise dominion over the animals (Genesis 1:27, 28).

David was amazed that God would exalt mankind to such a place of honor.

People tame and domesticate animals and use them for food (Genesis 9:3). While we must respect all life, human life is more valuable than animal life.

15. In what ways does mankind have dominion over the animal kingdom?

16. What are the implications for this dominion?

Praise the Lord!

David ended his psalm by restating its first phrase. This second use of the phrase is far weightier for us, since it follows the humbling truths laid out in the psalm.

17. Think about David's incredible life. What did it take for David to write such a psalm? Would he have penned it if he had been puffed up with pride about how important he was in God's program for Israel?

18. What effect would frequently reviewing this psalm have on a person?

Making It Personal

Though this psalm speaks of God's undeserved attention to mankind in general, we understand these thoughts from the perspective of God's personal attention and care for us.

19. What, if anything, have you consistently complained about recently? What makes you say, "I deserve better than this"?

20. What does complaining reveal about how a person views him- or herself in relation to God?

21. What are some instances of undeserved attention God has shown to you as a believer that you can focus on instead of complaining?

22. Now express your praise to the Lord for the undeserved attention He shows you. Write a prayer beginning with the words, "Lord, I do not deserve the attention and care You give me."

23. Take time to memorize Psalm 8:1.

God's Beneficial Word

*The Scriptures have wonderful effects
on our lives.*

Psalm 19

**"The law of the LORD is perfect, converting the
soul: the testimony of the LORD is sure, making
wise the simple. The statutes of the LORD are
right, rejoicing the heart: the commandment
of the LORD is pure, enlightening the eyes. The
fear of the LORD is clean, enduring for ever: the
judgments of the LORD are true and righteous
altogether" (Psalm 19:7–9).**

Since a growing percentage of people in the United States
are becoming senior citizens, the number of advertisements for prescription drugs has dramatically increased. All drug ads
have one thing in common: they all list the benefits of the drug before
listing the possible side effects. Imagine a commercial that starts with
these statements: "Our product may cause you to have dry mouth, hives,
swollen ankles, a massive heart attack, an eye explosion, or sudden limb
dismemberment. But don't worry about those side affects. Our product
can do wonderful things for you." The drug, no matter what its benefits,
would never sell. Change the same ad so it lists the benefits first and then
covers the risks in a fast, low voice, and customers would be willing to
overlook the risks (perhaps minus the heart attack, exploding eye, and
missing limbs) in order to enjoy the benefits. People want to know what
something can do for them before they hear about the side effects.

Getting Started

1. When, if ever, have you experienced a harmful side effect from a prescription drug?

2. What are three possible side effects that would probably keep you from trying a medication?

Searching the Scriptures

Psalm 19 lists the benefits of Scripture. However, unlike drug commercials, there are no risks tucked in at the end of the psalm. Scripture has only good side effects, or benefits. The benefits of Scripture should cause us to want to partake of it on a daily basis.

In the first six verses of this psalm, David was caught up with the revelation of God in the natural world. He then moved on to point out the benefits of the special revelation in Scripture.

God in Nature

The heavens and the skies are not empty. They contain the sun, moon, and stars—all of which reveal the glory of God. We see His "handiwork" in His created objects (v. 1). All during the day and night the heavenly bodies "speak" about God. The verb "uttereth" in verse 2 literally means "bubble forth." As a bubbling stream that continues to flow, so the heavens "bubble forth" the knowledge of God. The created bodies are continually speaking about God without saying a word!

Anthropologists calculate that there are about six thousand languages and dialects in the world. To each person who speaks one of these thousands of languages, God speaks His revelation through nature. It reaches all people and is equally intelligible to all. Whether a person speaks English, Spanish, or a dialect in a remote part of Africa, the revelation of God is "heard" (v. 3).

3. What can a person anywhere in the world know about God from nature?

4. What do Romans 1:19 and 20 say about nature's revealing knowledge about God?

David then gave a descriptive explanation of the sun. In the heavens God has established a place ("tabernacle") for the sun (Psalm 19:4). Each day the sun comes up and the sun goes down—from one end of the heavens to the other end (v. 6).

5. Read Psalm 19:5. What two picturesque images did David use to describe the circuit of the sun each day?

David concluded this section by commenting again on the extent of the revelation of God (v. 6). Just as no place escapes the heat of the sun, so no part of the world escapes the knowledge of God through the sun and the other heavenly bodies.

The Benefits of God's Word

As David mused on the revelation of God in the heavens (vv. 1–6), he thought of the greater and clearer revelation of God in the Scriptures and the beneficial effects of the Scriptures for believers (vv. 7–14).

David used six names for the Scriptures. While each name has a slightly different nuance from the others, together they are synonyms and are simply different ways to refer to the Scriptures. The "law" (v. 7) is more than a reference to the Mosaic law. It refers to all Scriptural truth. "Testimony" (v. 7) is God's witness or presentation of the truth. "Statutes" and "commandment" (v. 8) both indicate the responsibilities or decrees God gives to His people. "Fear of the LORD" (v. 9) is a name for God's Word that reflects an effect of God's Word—people learn to fear God through His Word (Deuteronomy 4:10). "Judgments" (Psalm 19:9) is a designation for God's judicial decisions. These six words show the comprehensive nature of God's Word.

6. Read through the descriptions of God's Word from Psalm 19:7–9 below. What observations can you make about the Scriptures from these descriptions?

> **Perfect**—flawless; complete
> **Sure**—reliable; trustworthy
> **Right**—morally straight; directs us in the right way
> **Pure**—no error; unadulterated; purifies
> **Clean**—without spot; cleanses
> **True**—dependable

The benefits of God's Word are incredible. We cannot help but be drawn to God's Word once we fully understand the benefits. David detailed them as follows:

Converting the soul—gives life to an unsaved person and revives a believer's weak spirit

Making wise the simple—gives wisdom to the humble at heart

Rejoicing the heart—encourages us no matter what the circumstances

Enlightening the eyes—gives guidance; brightens our lives and even our countenances

Enduring forever—will not lose its value; will not change, and therefore, gives confidence

Righteous altogether—leads to a righteous life

7. Which benefits of the Scriptures from Psalm 19:7–9 have you recently experienced?

8. Which of the benefits of God's Word means the most to you?

The Value of God's Word

Using imagery again (Psalm 19:10), David pointed out the value of Scripture by comparing it to the most valuable commodity (gold) and the sweetest food (honey) known to mankind at that time (119:72, 103). And he specifically identified "fine gold" (the purest and most valuable) and honey from the honeycomb (the sweetest kind). In essence, he said that the Scriptures are more valuable than the most valuable things you can think of and more desirable than the most desirable things you can want.

9. Fill in the following blanks with items that make the truth of Psalm 19:10 resound in your mind.

God's Word is more desirable than _____

and sweeter than _____

In verse 11 David identified two additional values of God's Word. First, David listed the value of being "warned" (v. 11). The Children of Israel had clear warnings from God. If they disobeyed Him, they would experience His righteous anger (Deuteronomy 6:10–16). God isn't being mean when He gives us warnings. Quite the opposite is true. His warnings are a benefit to us because they help us understand the seriousness of sin and because they motivate us to obey God. A mean God would hide the consequences of sin until He doled them out.

10. Read Hebrews 12:5–11. What general warning is included in this passage?

11. Read Acts 20:27–32 and Colossians 1:28 and 29. How seriously did Paul take his ministry to warn believers through God's Word?

12. What might Paul say to a pastor whose goal is to never upset anyone through his messages?

Second, obedience to God's Word brings the promise of blessing and reward (Psalm 19:11). Often God's clear warnings to the Children of Israel were accompanied by promises of blessings for their obedience (Deuteronomy 6:17–25). The principle of blessings for obedience carries over from the Old Testament into the New Testament. As part of God's church, we can't claim the promises God made to Israel, but God still blesses the obedient. Ultimately our blessings for obedience will come in eternity (2 Corinthians 5:10).

13. Read 2 Corinthians 5:9 and 10. What could be more desirable than hearing Christ say, "You did a great job as My servant. Great is your reward"?

The Responses to God's Word

The benefits and values of God's Word demand a response from us. We can't just agree that God's Word is beneficial and valuable. We have to do something with it. David's first response was to use God's Word to overcome sin.

In verse 12 David asked, "Who can understand his error?" The obvious answer to this rhetorical question is "no one." Our spiritual lives are complex. We don't even always know when we are sinning. "Secret faults" are unintentional sins that slip under our radar.

David knew God's Word could have a cleansing effect on him. He wanted God to use His Word to point out an unseen sin in his life.

14. What are some "secret sins" that God's Word will point out in our lives?

"Presumptuous sins" (v. 13) are sins blatantly committed. David wanted God to use His Word to break the obvious sin habits that had a hold on him. Hiding God's Word in our hearts is vital to overcoming our sin (Psalm 119:9–11). David concluded that the ministry of God through the Word would render him "upright," or blameless, and would help him to avoid much ("great") sin (Psalm 19:13).

15. What are some "presumptuous sins" that God's Word will point out in our lives?

David's second response to God's Word was to live pleasing to God. David wanted both his words and his thoughts to be acceptable to God (v. 14). In essence, David desired to replace old sinful habits with new words and thoughts that pleased the Lord. That David wanted his thoughts to be pleasing to God communicates his seriousness. God would renew David's words and thoughts as David spent time reading, studying, and meditating on God's Word.

16. Read Psalm 19:14. What two names did David call the Lord in the last part of this verse?

17. Why are those names important to anyone who tries to live out Psalm 19?

The benefits of the Scriptures listed in Psalm 19 form a package that cannot be matched anywhere else. We can have these beneficial effects in our lives as we spend time in the Scriptures and draw upon God's enabling strength.

Making It Personal

What has to happen for medicine or food to have their beneficial effects in us? We have to take it or eat it. What has to happen for the Scriptures to have their beneficial effects in our lives? We have to take the Word to ourselves. We need to let the Word of Christ dwell in us richly (Colossians 3:16).

18. Using the word "beneficial" as an acrostic, think of words or phrases that explain or describe how we receive these beneficial effects. The first one is done for you.

Believe the Word

E

N

E

F

I

C

I

A

L

19. What is your plan for staying in the Word every day? Write your present plan or what you would like to do.

Recommit yourself to be a person who spends time in the Word every day. Then you will see the wonderful benefits of God's Word in your life.

20. Take time to talk to the Lord about starting or recommitting to spend time in His Word daily.

21. Take time to memorize Psalm 19:7–9.

God's Abundant Provisions

God's provision for believers gives them satisfaction and rest.

Psalm 23

"The LORD is my shepherd; I shall not want. He maketh me to lie down in green pastures: he leadeth me beside the still waters. He restoreth my soul: he leadeth me in the paths of righteousness for his name's sake. Yea, though I walk through the valley of the shadow of death, I will fear no evil: for thou art with me; thy rod and thy staff they comfort me" (Psalm 23:1–4).

I'm a dog!" "I'm a lion! "I'm a dinosaur!" So go the cries of small children trying to better one another as they pretend they are animals. Children often select the loud and strong animals to imitate. Rarely will a child shout, "I'm a sheep!" For sheep are generally helpless, defenseless, and needy. Yet that is exactly what God calls us. We may not like being called sheep, but we can't deny how much we are like them. Psalm 23 explains in beautiful, meaningful imagery how our Good Shepherd provides the constant care that we, His sheep, so desperately need.

Getting Started

1. To what animal would you most like to be compared?

2. What do you think about being likened to a sheep?

Searching the Scriptures

Psalm 23 is probably the most well-known and well-loved of all psalms. Its imagery and simplicity make it meaningful to all believers. The strong note of faith in this psalm makes it a favorite.

In this psalm David used the imagery of a shepherd and sheep (vv. 1–4) and a host and guest (v. 5) to describe the Lord's abundant provisions. David concluded by expressing his confidence in the Lord for the remaining days of his life (v. 6).

Choosing a Shepherd

Shepherding was a common occupation in the ancient Near East. Shepherds were needed because sheep are weak, vulnerable animals that need someone to care for them. They probably could not survive without a shepherd to lead them to food and water and protect them from predators. In Old Testament times, shepherds lived with the flocks and were guides, physicians, and protectors.

3. Read John 10:1–18. What do you learn about shepherding from this passage?

Verses 1, 2

Verses 3–5

Verse 10, 11

Verse 14

When David called the Lord his shepherd, he wasn't just stating a fact. Rather he was communicating a decision he had made—a decision to *submit* to the Lord as his Shepherd.

4. What other shepherds could David have tried to follow even though he belonged to the Lord?

5. What are a few attributes or characteristics of the Lord that would especially be seen in His role as our Shepherd?

Content with My Shepherd

With a faithful shepherd, sheep did not lack anything. The shepherd provided all the food, water, rest, guidance, and even medical care the sheep needed. They had no needs the shepherd could not meet. Likewise, our Shepherd is unequivocally qualified to meet our every need—and He does.

Not only does our Shepherd meet our needs, He also makes us content with what we have. Paul learned to be content no matter how much he had (Philippians 4:10–13).

Some sheep can be led to lush green pastures but still not be content. They constantly look for a chance to escape to what they think are greener pastures. When they do get away, they often end up in a field with grass inferior to that of the field they left. But their discontentment keeps them from returning to the lush field their shepherd selected for them. They want to control where they go and what they eat. They want to be their own shepherd.

As believers, we must guard against discontentment. We live in a world whose economy thrives on dissatisfied consumers. "I want it bigger, better, faster, stronger!" is their cry. Answering that cry is big business. The electronics industry alone has boomed by making better, faster, and more efficient devices.

6. What are some other evidences that we live in a discontent, longing society?

7. How does a believer's discontentment with the Lord as his or her Shepherd show up in that believer's life?

Secure Enough to Lie Down

Sheep need to feel safe and secure before they will lie down. To them, lying down means making their only hope of escape from enemies, running, that much harder to do. A prone sheep is easy prey for lurking predators. But the shepherd's presence and watchful eyes give the sheep a feeling of safety and security. Sheep will lie down in the presence of their shepherd.

We can be secure no matter what our circumstances. Our Shepherd is near. His presence will bring us rest.

8. What does it normally take for you to relax and sleep well at night?

Knowing that the Lord is our Shepherd should allow us to sleep well every night. His constant vigilance and all-knowing eyes are comforting to those in His fold.

Following My Leader

The shepherd knew his sheep needed water, so he led them to a place of still, or quiet, waters. Sheep often recoil from moving waters. They are perhaps fearful that the rushing waters may sweep them away. They also have trouble drinking from a moving stream without the water rushing up their noses. The shepherd, sensitive to his sheep's needs, found springs where the water was quiet so the sheep could rest while they drank.

God knows what we need, and He leads us in order to meet those needs.

9. Read Psalm 23:3. What is implied by the phrase, "He restoreth my soul"?

"All we like sheep have gone astray" sums up all of mankind (Isaiah 53:6). We retain our propensity to wander from the Lord even after our salvation. When we wander, we get into trouble. We eventually get discouraged and feel defeated.

10. Read Proverbs 14:12. How does the truth of this verse relate to our propensity to wander from our Shepherd and His leading?

Our Shepherd will restore our souls and set us again on the right paths—"the paths of righteousness" (Psalm 23:3). The word for "path" refers to ways clearly marked by frequent traffic. The paths of righteousness are not a mystery to the Lord's sheep. His Word points the way to these paths and makes them very clear.

These paths that our Shepherd leads us on are paths of blessing.
He always wants the best for us. That doesn't mean we will all be rich
and live in ease. God's blessings have little to do with money and circumstances. His blessings are in the form of spiritual fortitude, enabling
grace, growth in understanding, and spiritual refreshment.

The Lord restores us and leads us in paths of righteousness "for his
name's sake" (v. 3). Our lives reflect on our Shepherd. We are examples
of God's care for His own.

11. What would an unbeliever think of the Lord as a shepherd if His
sheep were skittish and thin from walking on their own paths?

As the Lord's sheep, we ought to stand out rather than blend in.
Those who don't belong to the Lord's flock ought to be asking us,
"Who's your Shepherd? How can I meet Him? Does He have any more
room in His fold?"

Through the Valley

The "valley of the shadow of death" (v. 4) is literally "the valley of
deep darkness." Sometimes the right path on which the shepherd led
the sheep wound through a deep valley filled with dark shadows. If
ever a sheep felt vulnerable, it was in a shadowy valley. The possibility
of predators in the intermittent darkness frightened the sheep.

David could identify with dark valleys. He had led sheep through
them and had figuratively gone through them as a sheep.

12. What have been the darkest valleys you have gone through?

13. What frightened you most about your darkest valleys? Was it the
unknown? an inability to control the situation?

David didn't fear the evil of the dark valleys, for his Shepherd was with him. When we think of a flock of sheep going through a valley with just one shepherd, it is easy to see that the sheep would still be uneasy. Their shepherd couldn't practically help all the sheep simultaneously. But David pictured the Lord walking through the valley by his side as if David were the only sheep the Lord had to take care of.

We each get all of the attention the Lord, our Shepherd, could possibly give us. He is not torn between protecting one sheep or another through a valley. That is the beauty of an infinite God! He personally holds our hands as He leads us through the valley. We don't need to worry that God is too busy to deal with our struggles and fears. He will answer and help every believer who comes to Him as if that believer is the only person crying out to Him.

The shepherd's rod and staff brought David even more comfort. A rod was a short club shepherds used to defend the sheep (1 Samuel 17:35). The staff was a longer stick with a curved top used to control the sheep, either in discipline or for protection. These two tools symbolized the Lord's abilities to help. The Lord never has to tell one of His sheep, "I really wish I could help, but I just am not able to." We can trust that God is able to help us through the valley.

Often a flock of sheep would emerge from a valley and travel on to higher elevations that were lush with green pastures. In this way the valleys were a pathway to blessing.

14. What blessings came as a result of the dark valleys you have walked through with the Lord?

The Lord's Dinner Guest

David then switched metaphors and portrayed the Lord as his gracious host. The Lord figuratively welcomed David to a well-set banquet table. The enemies looked on helplessly while David enjoyed the Lord's safety and hospitality.

15. Imagine a banquet table set in the middle of a modern war zone. What two words come to your mind at such a thought?

As guests entered an ancient Near Eastern banquet, the host might anoint them with oil to show they were welcomed, honored guests (cf. Psalm 45:7; 92:10; 133:2; Luke 7:46). The oil had a pleasant fragrance and smooth touch. The result was a refreshed feeling like what we get from taking a shower. The anointing was a special touch to show love and care.

The overflowing cup showed the host's gracious manner of entertainment and his generosity toward his guest. He wanted his guests to have the best drink available and plenty of it. A cup filled to the rim told the guests that they could have as much to drink as they wanted. The modern equivalent is a bottomless cup of coffee.

16. Read John 10:10. How does this verse relate to Psalm 23:5?

David's Response of Faith

After exalting in the Lord's goodness as a shepherd and host, David concluded with a statement of strong faith in the future (Psalm 23:6). David spoke confidently that the Lord's "goodness and mercy" would vigorously pursue him the rest of his life. The Lord's goodness meets our needs, and His mercy withholds the retribution that we deserve for our sins.

The fact that goodness and mercy *follow* us is significant. For even if we wander from the path of righteousness, the Lord's goodness and mercy follow on our heels to work to restore us to the path.

David considered the Lord's sanctuary, where God's presence dwelt, to be his home (Psalms 27:4; 65:4). In this verse he expressed his desire to dwell in the Lord's house the remaining years of his life to enjoy communion with the Lord.

As believers today, we understand that the Lord's presence is not in a place but in each believer. We should desire to have intimate communion with the Lord right now, and we look forward to communing forever with Him in Heaven.

Making It Personal

Reading Psalm 23 ought to bring a smile to your soul. There is nothing you lack with the Lord as your Shepherd and gracious Host. Will you, like David, submit to the Lord, your Shepherd?

17. What in your life right now seems too big for you to handle?

18. Tell your Shepherd about your troubles. Ask Him for His help.

Trust your Shepherd! There is no other one Who would or could care for you as Jesus does.

19. Take time to memorize Psalm 23:1–4.

Living Confidently

*Believers can be confident and calm
in frightening times.*

Psalm 27

**"The LORD is my light and my salvation; whom
shall I fear? the LORD is the strength of my life;
of whom shall I be afraid?" (Psalm 27:1).**

Twenty-first-century life offers a host of conveniences
ranging from handheld electronic gadgets to robotic
vacuums. Modern technology establishes instant communication around
the globe, delivers a wealth of information almost instantly, enhances
our driving experiences, improves medical diagnoses and surgical proce-
dures, makes it possible to shop without leaving home, and even makes
a trip to the dentist almost pleasant.

However, technology has a downside. We face potentially devastating harm at the hands of enemies who might use nuclear, chemical, and
biological agents against us. Understandably, fear grips many of our fellow citizens.

David lived three thousand years before the twenty-first century,
but he, too, lived in frightening times. Internal strife troubled Israel, and
nearby nations posed a constant threat. As for David personally, he was
a marked man. His enemies tracked him as relentlessly as a pack of
ravenous wolves tracks a deer. But as we learn from Psalm 27, he re-
mained confident and calm.

Getting Started

1. What are some popular means of handling uncertain situations?

2. How do you often handle uncertain situations?

Searching the Scriptures

A consensus of opinion among Bible teachers places the writing of Psalm 27 during David's exile from home, when King Saul searched for him in the nooks and crannies of the wilderness. Saul's ultimate goal was to kill David and thereby eliminate his rival to the throne.

Confidence from Who God Is

David laid the foundation for his psalm by describing God as his light, salvation, and strength. As David's light, God illuminated David's heart and path. David personally knew God and was directed by God to live in the truth. The apostle John picked up this theme in his Gospel when he called Jesus "the true Light" (John 1:1–9). Without the light of Christ, no one would come to the Father and realize salvation from sin.

As David's "salvation," God was David's deliverer and rescuer. In the immediate sense God rescued David from his enemies. In the broader sense God rescued David from his sin. God is still in the rescuing business. When Simeon lifted up the Christ Child in the temple, he said, "Mine eyes have seen thy salvation, which thou hast prepared before the face of all people; a light to lighten the Gentiles, and the glory of thy people Israel" (Luke 2:30–32). Through faith in Christ we can each claim with David, "God is my salvation." After salvation, God is our deliverer, Who goes with us through the trials of life.

God was also David's "strength," or "stronghold." God was a safe place that kept David from fearing his enemies. David found rejuvenation and strength in God.

Our salvation is not just to secure our destiny. It also sustains us until we get there. God solves our sin problem, but then He continues to supply the light, deliverance, and strength we need as we live for Him. As believers, we ought to move confidently through life with the help of God's light, salvation, and strength.

3. Read Psalm 27:1. What did David conclude based on the fact that God was his light, salvation, and strength?

4. How do these three identifications of God from verse 1 apply to your life?

Because the Lord is my light

Because the Lord is my salvation

Because the Lord is my strength (stronghold)

Confidence from What God Has Done

Undoubtedly David's confidence in the Lord resulted in part from observing what the Lord had done for him already. Verse 2 recalls a resounding victory in which David's enemies "stumbled and fell" when they attacked him. If we reflect on the Lord's care of us in the past, we will trust Him to protect us when future crises emerge.

Even the threat of a vast array of enemies encamped against David would not shake David's confidence in the Lord. Not even an outbreak of full-scale war against him would weaken his trust in the Lord (v. 3). No enemy is so fierce that the Lord cannot triumph over it, and no set of circumstances is so oppressive that the Lord's grace cannot penetrate

it. Like David, the prophet Elisha was confident in God because of what
God had done in the past. Elisha's confidence in God in the midst of
turmoil was exemplary (2 Kings 6:11–23).

5. Read 2 Kings 6:11–23. What assurance did Elisha give his servant
as they faced the Syrian army?

6. According to verses 17 and 18, what spiritual resource did Elisha
employ?

7. Read Ephesians 6:16 and 1 John 5:4. What spiritual resource can
you use to overcome assaults launched by the Devil and his followers?

Confidence in What God Will Do

David was a fugitive in the wilderness, but his heart was in the
house of the Lord, where he longed to dwell all the days of his life.
There he would worship the Lord and seek His guidance (Psalm 27:4).
No place on earth seemed safer and sweeter (v. 5). Not even a comfortable palace appealed to David as much as the Lord's tabernacle.

8. Read Psalm 27:6. What would David's worship in the tabernacle
include?

The "joy" in verse 6 refers to "joyous shouts." David planned to get
excited about God and to let all those around him know about God's
work on his behalf.

9. What did David's plans to praise God before he was even delivered from his enemies say about his confidence in God?

10. When has the Lord done something for you that made you want to shout His praises?

11. How did you praise God at that time?

Confident Prayer

David was not only a man of praise but also a man of prayer. He implored the Lord to hear his prayer and grant him mercy (v. 7). He responded to the Lord's invitation to pray by turning his heart toward the Lord (v. 8).

It seems David faced imminent danger. Perhaps Saul and his men were bearing down on him. Further, David may have offended the Lord in some way and feared the Lord might not come to his rescue. He prayed, therefore, "Hide not thy face far from me; put not thy servant away in anger" (v. 9). Once again he recounted the Lord's deliverance in the past and urged the Lord not to leave him in the lurch. His confidence in the Lord may have sagged a bit, but he quickly strengthened it by calling the Lord the God of his salvation and by testifying that the Lord's care of him exceeded even that of his parents (v. 10).

Following the Lord's will was David's paramount concern, so he prayed for guidance. He asked the Lord to lead him "in a plain path" because of his enemies (v. 11). "A plain path" refers to a route that is free of traps and ambushes. The Lord can prepare such a way for us, too, when danger lurks nearby.

David was wise. He realized that past victory does not guarantee future victories. He prayed for divine deliverance from lying enemies who had sworn to kill him (v. 12). Commenting on verse 12, Charles Haddon Spurgeon observed, "Slander is an old-fashioned weapon out of the armory of hell and is still in plentiful use; and no matter how holy a man may be. There will be some who will defame him. It is their vital breath to hate the good" (*Treasury of David* [Grand Rapids: Zondervan Publishing House, 1940], 138).

12. What will happen to God's servants if their confidence rises and falls on what others say and think about them?

The Lord had chosen David to be Israel's king, and He eventually delivered David from Saul and his followers and placed him on the throne (2 Samuel 5:1–5, 12). So Saul could not have destroyed David. No one ever wins a battle against God.

But occasionally evildoers kill believers. The blood of martyrs flows from the history of the church. Courageous Stephen became the church's first martyr after he testified for Christ to an angry mob (Acts 7:54–60). James, the brother of John, met martyrdom at the hands of Herod (12:1, 2). The apostle Paul, too, died as a martyr. These men of faith blazed a trail of martyrdom thousands of missionaries and other faithful Christians have followed through the centuries. However, they were all victors. Through Christ, they triumphed over their persecutors by exercising resolute faith and by drawing upon all-sufficient grace. They had completed their divinely commissioned work on earth and then passed into Heaven to be with Christ and receive a victor's crown.

13. Why is the center of God's will the safest place to be?

While David dodged his enemies in the wilderness, he never lost sight of God's goodness. He would have "fainted"—faltered and fallen—

if he had not "believed to see the goodness of the LORD in the land of the living" (Psalm 27:13). David must have remembered that the Lord had promised to make him king and therefore would not let him die in the wilderness. The Lord is good, and He always keeps His word.

It has been said that the Lord is never early but that He is always on time. David was willing to wait on the Lord to fulfill His will in His good time. David counseled (perhaps his followers) to wait on the Lord and to be of good courage, believing the Lord would strengthen their hearts (v. 14).

14. What would you tell a believer who claims he or she can't help but chronically worry?

Waiting is hard work for many of us. We live in a time of instant messages and instant potatoes, but the Lord's best blessings come to those who wait on Him. Hebrews 6:12 admonishes us to be "followers of them who through faith and patience inherit the promises." Faith and patience characterized David and other heroes of the faith. If these qualities abide in us, we will surely handle fear in a way that honors the Lord and brings rich blessings to us.

Making It Personal

Today life is lived in the fast lane: nothing remains the same for long. Unfortunately even many of us Christians can nod our agreement with the Pennsylvania Dutch saying, "We get too soon old and too late smart." Because life is short yet full of challenges, we need to follow David's example and face our fears with confident faith, prayer, and patience.

15. What threatens your confidence in the Lord?

16. Write a prayer committing your fears to the Lord, knowing He will not fail you.

17. Whom can you encourage to live confidently through a particularly difficult circumstance?

18. Memorize Psalm 27:1.

Confessing Sins

Confession of sins is crucial to spiritual growth.

Psalm 51

"Create in me a clean heart, O God; and renew a right spirit within me. . . . Restore unto me the joy of thy salvation; and uphold me with thy free spirit" (Psalm 51:10, 12).

Not long ago, an eBay ad offered a truly unusual antique for the home that has everything. It was a hand-carved oak confessional from around 1880. It had been removed from the Church of St. Charles in Algiers, Algeria. The asking price was two thousand dollars.

Perhaps a buyer would use the confessional as a backyard playhouse or a coat closet. If nothing else, the confessional would serve to remind the buyer to confess his or her sins on a regular basis—not that confessionals have anything to do with God or true confession of sins.

Like that antique confessional, genuine, contrite, Biblically directed confession itself seems to be almost archaic. Perhaps we have bought so thoroughly into the positive self-image, feel-good-about-yourself philosophy that we fail to acknowledge our sins and the need to confess them to the Lord.

After being confronted by God through Nathan the prophet, David cried out to God and confessed his sins. He recorded his heartfelt words for us in Psalm 51.

Getting Started

1. How often should believers confess their sins?

2. What might you gain from studying David's confession of sin?

Searching the Scriptures

The Lord called David "a man after mine own heart" (Acts 13:22), but David was not perfect. He had a sin nature, just as we have. After serving and worshiping God devotedly for many years, David caved in to temptation. From the rooftop of his palace, he cast a lustful eye on Bathsheba, who was bathing on a neighboring rooftop. That incident led David into a series of sins that stabbed his conscience and flooded his soul with guilt.

3. Read 2 Samuel 11. What sins did David commit?

4. Read 2 Samuel 12:1–14. In whose sight had David sinned (v. 9)?

5. What consequences of sin would David face (vv. 10–12)?

6. How did David respond to Nathan's message (v. 13)?

Psalm 51 records David's contrite confession to the Lord. The word "confess" means "to say the same thing." When we confess sins, we are adopting God's attitude about sin. God despises sin and sees it as a horrific offense against Him, and we should too. He sees sin as inconsistent with righteousness, and we should too.

David did not ignore his guilt. Nor did he minimize his guilt or blame his sinning on circumstances or others. He took full responsibility for his sin and poured out his heart to God in confession.

7. Why will blaming parents or past experiences for one's present sin never lead to victory and forgiveness from God?

David appealed to God for forgiveness based on His loving-kindness and the multitude of His "tender mercies" (Psalm 51:1). David knew he didn't deserve forgiveness, but he also knew that God is loving and merciful.

Sins Blotted Out

In Old Testament times a debt was cancelled by erasing it rather than by writing a new certificate saying the debt has been paid. David desired a blotting out of, or a permanent erasing of, his transgressions from God's record book. The word "transgressions" refers to the willful disobedience of God's laws.

God wanted David to request that his sins be blotted out, for God is not reluctant to forgive sin. Imagine your sins listed on a whiteboard with God standing with an eraser poised to wipe away your sins as soon as you confess them. First John 1:9 supports such an image. It says, "If we confess our sins, he is faithful and just to forgive us our sins, and to cleanse us from all unrighteousness." God will erase all of the sins we confess. None of our sins are written in permanent ink.

A believer's *salvation* from sin is never at stake. All our sins are forever covered by the blood of Christ (Colossians 2:13, 14). But the sins we commit as believers do break down the fellowship we enjoy with the Father. We cannot grow in Christ if we fail to confess our sins to God.

8. How does the picture of God waiting to wipe away your sins affect your perspective on confessing your sin?

Sins Washed Away

David went on to ask God to wash him thoroughly from his iniquity (Psalm 51:2). In essence, he asked God to do the work of a fuller, or a dyer of cloth. Before a fuller could dye a new piece of cloth, he had to remove the oils and gooey matters from it. He did this by treading the cloth by foot or by beating it with a stick. David saw his iniquity, flagrant violations of God's standards, as the oily and gooey stuff that God needed to remove from his heart.

In his Gospel, Mark referred to a fuller's work when he wrote about Jesus on the Mount of Transfiguration. He said that Christ's "raiment became shining, exceeding white as snow; so as no fuller on earth can white them" (Mark 9:3). Jesus, Who is absolutely devoid of sin, shined brightly before Peter, James, and John.

David's sin had made him "dirty." He wanted God to make him clean and useful again. As we reflect on our sin, we might conclude that God doesn't want us anymore. So we avoid God, believing He would never listen to us again—much less wash the sin from our lives. David had no such inhibitions. He confessed his sin, and God stripped the "oily and gooey matters" from his life.

9. Have you ever felt as if God wouldn't want you anymore because of something you did? How did you respond?

10. How does the picture of the fuller whitening a cloth help you to understand God's response to your confession of sins?

Not once did David refer to his sin as simply a mistake. His sin caused him to feel defiled, and it constantly occupied his attention (Psalm 51:3). He saw his sin as God saw it.

Although he had sinned against Bathsheba, her husband, and the nation, David recognized that he had sinned first and foremost against God. If he had not sinned against God, he would not have wronged others. He was aware that God was justified in exposing and judging his sin (v. 4). He admitted that he had been a sinner from his conception and that the only way to solve his sin problem was to have a change of heart (vv. 5, 6). David recognized that he was totally depraved and that God was the only solution to his sin problem.

Once again David cried out for cleansing. He asked the Lord to "purge," or cleanse, him with "hyssop." Hyssop was a plant used in Old Testament cleansing ceremonies, particularly in cleansing a leper or a person who had touched a dead body (Leviticus 14:6, 7; Numbers 19:18). David's transgressions had made him feel unclean on the inside, but the Lord would make David "whiter than snow" (Psalm 51:7).

Effects of Sin

11. Sin had negatively affected David's whole being. According to the following verses in Psalm 51, what parts of David's being did sin negatively affect?

Verse 8

Verse 8

Verse 10

12. Have you ever felt so burdened by sin that it affected your health? What did you do to relieve the burden?

David's guilt had robbed him of joy and gladness, and it had also harmed him physically (v. 8). He implored the Lord to look no longer on his sins, and once again he prayed that the Lord would blot out all his iniquities (v. 9).

David wasn't repeating his request that God would blot out his sins because he doubted that God had heard him. Rather he was demonstrating his humility and communicating his trust that God was the answer to his sin problem. God was the only One Who could create a clean heart and renew a "right," or steadfast, spirit in him (v. 10).

New Way of Living

A clean heart would align David's thinking, planning, and decision making with God's will. A steadfast spirit would keep David fixed on God's way. In other words, David wasn't looking just for relief from his sin; he was looking for a new way of thinking and living. He wanted to again be a man after God's own heart.

13. What will most likely happen to a person who confesses his or her sin but then doesn't make any effort to change? (See Ephesians 4:21–24.)

David understood that sin separates the sinner from God and is incompatible with the Holy Spirit. Therefore he prayed that the Lord would not remove His Holy Spirit from him (Psalm 51:11). God had rejected King Saul because of his sinful heart (1 Samuel 13:13, 14). David didn't want God to do the same with him.

Like Saul, believers today can be set aside by God and no longer used in certain ministry capacities (cf. 1 Corinthians 9:27). But we don't have to worry about losing the Holy Spirit.

14. Read John 14:16 and 17 and Ephesians 1:13. Why would it be inappropriate for a Christian to echo David's prayer in Psalm 51:11?

15. Read Psalm 51:12. How might this verse help someone who feels utterly distraught over a sin he or she has committed?

Renewed Joy and Service

Forgiven, David again asked God to restore to him his joy (v. 12). That request seems simple, but remember that David was guilty of murder. The guilty feelings from murdering a loyal man like Uriah would have threatened to drag David into a depressed state for the rest of his life. In verse 14 David even asked the Lord to deliver him from the *guilt* of bloodshed. He could have easily concluded that he didn't deserve to experience joy ever again—and he would have been right. But God is gracious. David's request to be upheld by God's "free," or generous, Spirit enlisted God's gracious help in keeping David from a life of depression (v. 12). Joy is possible after sin, but only through total dependence on God's generous Spirit.

Not only could David experience renewed joy, but he could also be used by God to help fellow transgressors (v. 13). David's testimony about how God blotted out his sin and restored his joy would deeply impact transgressors who felt the same weight of sin that David had felt. Perhaps David's testimony and his singing of praises to God were linked (vv. 14, 15). It is not out of the realm of possibility that David wrote Psalm 51 to sing it to transgressors and thereby teach them God's ways.

16. How do you normally respond to personal testimonies about how God delivered people from their sin? Do you focus on how great God is or on how rotten the people were?

17. What might happen in a church if more members were honest about how God has freed them from sin?

For believers to tell others about their sins and how God restored them to His side takes broken hearts. A heart filled with pride would never allow such an admittance. David had such a contrite, humble heart—the kind of heart God wanted him to have.

Proper Sacrifice

Neither large contributions given to one's church nor sacrificial acts of Christian service can substitute for contrite confession of sin. David was rich enough to offer thousands of animals as sacrifices to the Lord, but he knew God would reject such sacrifices if David's heart was not right with Him (v. 16). The only sacrifice God will accept is "a broken and a contrite heart" (v. 17).

Apparently David had begun to repair Jerusalem's walls to strengthen the city's defenses against her enemies. His sins must have removed his focus from this task, leaving Jerusalem vulnerable to attack. So David asked the Lord, "Build thou the walls of Jerusalem" (v. 18).

Psalm 51 ends with the acknowledgment that God would be pleased with David's sacrifices and burnt offerings once David's heart was right with Him (v. 19). True worship rises from a heart that is clean and free of guilt.

Making It Personal

18. Assess your relationship to the Lord. Have you allowed a sin to drive a wedge between you and the Lord?

19. Confess your sin to the Lord. Write a prayer similar to David's prayer, asking God to blot out your sins and to cleanse your heart.

Don't ever put off confessing sins. Deal with them immediately. Also set aside a time each day to confess any sins that you left unconfessed during the day.

20. David knew that forgiveness and restoration would bring back the joy of his salvation. Do you feel burdened by guilt even though you have confessed your sins? Pray for the restoration of your joy.

21. Rejoice! You are forgiven and free from the burden of your sin. Write a prayer of praise to God, and remember to praise Him every day!

22. Memorize Psalm 51:10 and 12.

Lesson 7

The Enemy Called Envy

God's abiding presence is better than abundant property.

Psalm 73

**"Whom have I in heaven but thee? and there is none upon earth that I desire beside thee. My flesh and my heart faileth: but God is the strength of my heart, and my portion for ever"
(Psalm 73:25, 26).**

D ad, can I get a Game Boy?" asked Jack, age seven. "All my friends have one."

"Would that really make you happy?" the dad asked in return.

"Oh, yes! I wouldn't want anything else if I got a Game Boy."

Patiently the dad continued his conversation with his son by explaining that having what other people have would never make him happy. He would always want more.

The dad was speaking from experience. He had often dreamed of a vacation home in Florida and one in the mountains of Colorado, a zippy sports car, a padded bank account, and a huge house with a pristine yard and glorious fountains. There are people who have all of those things and more. For the dad, being envious of them is a natural reaction. But when he focuses on God and the treasure that he has in Him, the envy dissipates into sweet satisfaction.

Psalm 73 talks about envy and our propensity to get swallowed up in an I-want-what-they-have cycle. All of us will do well to study the psalm and break that cycle by finding our satisfaction in God.

Getting Started

1. What signs of envy have you seen in young children?

2. What signs of envy have you seen in yourself?

Searching the Scriptures

Psalm 73 is the personal story of Asaph's struggle with envy and how he gained victory over it. We, too, become envious occasionally. We may envy a person who drives the car we would like to own or lives in a house that is far beyond our price range or holds a high-salaried position. Therefore, Asaph's psalm carries a significant message for us.

3. Read 1 Chronicles 16:4 and 5 and 2 Chronicles 29:30. What ministries did Asaph have?

Good Theology, Nagging Question

Asaph's theology was fine. He believed God was good to His people (Psalm 73:1). The history of Israel proved that notion.

4. What did God do for Israel, particularly early in her history, that proved God's goodness to the people of Israel?

Asaph confessed in Psalm 73:2 that he had almost tumbled into a backslidden position. When he said that his "feet were almost gone," he meant that he was staggering around and about to fall. When Asaph said his "steps had well nigh slipped," he meant that he was off the beaten, secure path and on treacherous ground. The picture is of Asaph burdened by questions about life. These pressing questions were nearly his downfall.

Though Asaph knew in his heart that God is good, he envied the prosperous wicked (v. 3). He could not understand why God allowed them to enjoy the "good life." They seemed to possess good health (v. 4). The word "bands," or pains, in verse 4 signifies that the wicked seemed to die without experiencing a painful disease or a slow, agonizing death. They lived and died with ease. The phrase "their strength is firm" refers to the lasting strength they enjoyed throughout their lives. They were not troubled as other men were (v. 5).

5. Read Psalm 73:3–6. Was Asaph's perception of the wicked entirely accurate? Were all the wicked people exceptionally healthy, strong, and trouble free? Explain.

6. a. What does an envious attitude do to our perception of those we envy?

b. Do we see them as they are, or do we tend to see only what will build our case?

Asaph's experiences must have contrasted sharply with those of the prosperous wicked. When he looked at his own life, he saw rough seas, but when he looked at the lives of the wicked, he saw smooth sailing. What he perceived didn't seem to support his belief that God is good to His people.

Perhaps our perspective parallels Asaph's. We know God is good. We know, too, that "all things work together for good to them that love God, to them who are the called according to his purpose" (Romans 8:28). Nevertheless, we may find it difficult to align our theology and life experiences. We ask why God allows hardship and suffering to buffet us while everything seems to go so well for many profane unbelievers. Envy seizes us and threatens our relationship with God. We, like Asaph, focus only on the wicked who seem to be living trouble free.

Characteristics of the Wicked

Asaph described the wicked from his perspective, starting in verse 6. The first characteristic he noticed was their pride. The wicked were not ashamed of their pride. They wore it as their "chain," or necklace. They were proud of their pride.

Second, Asaph noted that "violence covereth them as a garment" (v. 6). The wicked showed off their violence as if it were a piece of fine clothing. Their prosperity gave them power, which they abused by being harsh and aggressive.

Third, the writer observed that the wicked had bulging eyes from their "fatness," or abundance. They had a lot and boasted that they couldn't even wish for the abundance they had (v. 7).

Fourth, Asaph noticed that the wicked used their mouths to brag about evil, threaten oppression, and scoff at righteousness (v. 8).

Fifth, the wicked brazenly denied God's abilities and place in Heaven. Their dominance of those they oppressed and the seeming lack of reprisal from God for their actions gave them boldness to speak against God.

Finally, "their tongue walketh through the earth" (v. 9). In other words, they recruited people to their line of reasoning.

7. Read Psalm 73:6–9. Which of the characteristics of the wicked have you seen most predominantly in society? Explain.

8. How do the wicked most effectively recruit people to their line of reasoning today?

Understanding the exact meaning of verse 10 is difficult. Some scholars believe that by seeing the prosperous, smooth lifestyle of the wicked, many of God's people concluded it didn't pay to serve God. Consequently they embraced the sinful ways of the wicked. Others believe the verse is referring to the persecution of God's people by the wicked. The latter interpretation probably is better, since it fits with the immediate context.

The wicked claimed God didn't know what was taking place on earth (v. 11). After all, they reasoned, they prospered, whereas the saints suffered (v. 12).

At the height of his confusion about the wicked, Asaph reasoned that the internal cleansing of his heart and the external cleansing of his hands were worthless (v. 13). He was plagued and chastened while the wicked prospered. God didn't seem to be helping him (v. 14). Asaph knew that if he voiced his thoughts, he would harm God's people (v. 15). So he kept silent and continued to ponder the question of the prosperity of the wicked. Asaph couldn't come up with a solution. He tried to reason his way to an answer, but all he got was a colossal headache (v. 16).

An Answer at Last

Asaph finally found the answer he needed by going to the tabernacle. The tabernacle was the "sanctuary of God" in Asaph's lifetime. For us, it represents the place of prayer and Biblical meditation. Often, even our pastors and Christian friends try but fail to give us the answer we crave when life seems unfair. But when we get alone with God, we begin to see the situation from His perspective (v. 17).

9. Read Psalm 73:18–20. Describe the ultimate end of the wicked.

10. Which of the perceived benefits of the wicked are weighty enough to make up for the end of the wicked (vv. 3–5)?

After gaining a clear picture of God's plan for the wicked, Asaph felt convicted (v. 21). He realized that his doubt demonstrated a lack of spiritual understanding. He had acted in a "foolish" and "ignorant" manner. He had shown no more spiritual awareness of God's character and ways than an animal would have (v. 22).

Perhaps every believer at one time or another judges a situation from a purely human perspective. We may perceive material prosperity as the good life and envy those who have it. But the truly good life is built on God's Word, not on the things of the world.

Having come to his spiritual senses, Asaph counted his blessings. He knew that the wicked would perish (v. 27), but he had treasures that money couldn't buy and trials couldn't destroy.

God was continually with Asaph and was holding his right hand (v. 23). Undoubtedly he shared the conviction David expressed in Psalm 23:4: "Yea, though I walk through the valley of the shadow of death, I will fear no evil: for thou art with me; thy rod and thy staff they comfort me." It is better to have God in one's life than to have all the wealth of the world without Him.

11. Read Hebrews 13:5. Why should the believer be content instead of covetous?

Asaph deemed divine guidance a rich treasure. He knew God would guide him through life and then welcome him "to glory" (Psalm 73:24). We, too, can spend our days in the will of God and look forward to a glorious entrance into Heaven. These benefits lie out of the reach of the richest people on earth if they fail to trust in Christ.

Jesus related the story of a rich man who "was clothed in purple and fine linen, and fared sumptuously every day" and a beggar named Lazarus who was "full of sores" (Luke 16:19–25). The beggar was so impoverished that he longed for "the crumbs which fell from the rich man's table." But when the men died, the rich man experienced the torments of Hell, whereas the poor man enjoyed the comforts of Paradise. When the rich man begged Abraham to dispatch Lazarus to dip his finger in water and cool his tongue, Abraham declined. "Son," he said, "remember that thou in thy lifetime receivedst thy good things, and likewise Lazarus evil things: but now he is comforted, and thou art tormented." The prosperous wicked eventually exchange temporal luxury for eternal misery!

Desire for God Alone

We may sing about our mansion in Heaven, but our greatest delight should be that of meeting the Lord there. Asaph's eye of faith was focused on the God of Heaven, and Asaph desired no one on earth except God (Psalm 73:25). His health might decline, but God was the strength of his heart and his portion forever (v. 26). No longer envious of the wicked, Asaph was content to entrust his life to God. He had found that the best things in life are not things.

12. Read 1 Timothy 6:6–10. What did Paul teach Timothy about envy and contentment?

13. How can a believer take his or her eyes off the things of this life and fix them on eternal things?

Asaph concluded Psalm 73 with another mention of the judgment that awaits the wicked (v. 27) and an exclamation of the benefit of drawing near to God (v. 28). He had put his trust in the Lord God and was prepared to declare all His works.

14. What happens to the arrogant boasting of the wicked when believers start to talk about their God and His wondrous works?

When we are tempted to harbor envy, we should draw near to God, as Asaph did. And like Asaph, we will find God worthy of our trust. Having drawn near to God and having put our trust in Him, we, too, will be positioned well to declare His works.

Making It Personal

Envy is almost as old as human history, and it has robbed many believers of true contentment and joy. However, we can defeat this monster by drawing near to God and counting our blessings.

15. Determine what you have valued the most on your life journey by answering the following questions:

What do you spend your time on?

What do you spend you money on?

16. What blessings has the Lord given you that are worth far more than material possessions?

17. What do you find most appealing about Heaven?

18. Memorize Psalm 73:25 and 26.

Life Is Short; Use It Wisely

God expects believers to take full advantage of opportunities to serve Him.

Psalm 90

"So teach us to number our days, that we may apply our hearts unto wisdom" (Psalm 90:12).

Whether we care to admit it or not, life passes quickly, and we receive not-so-subtle messages that we are not as young as we used to be. A message to this effect may bounce at us from a lingering look in a mirror. It may come in the form of another pill to take in a growing list of prescriptions. It may reach us on a tennis court or on a hiking trail. We simply don't move as quickly and as pain free as we used to, and we tire sooner. Or a class reunion may convince us that life is fleeting. A former classmate may ask, "What happened to that full head of hair you sported in high school?" Or another may remark, "How did we gain so much weight? Remember how skinny we were?"

Getting old definitely isn't for sissies!

Getting Started

1. What makes you realize that life is brief?

2. How can you make the so-called sunset years bright?

Searching the Scriptures

Psalm 90 may be the oldest psalm. Moses wrote it as a prayer during Israel's travels in the wilderness. Perhaps he wrote it after the Israelites refused to enter the Promised Land (Numbers 13; 14) and were sentenced by the Lord to wander in the wilderness for forty years until that faithless generation had passed away. In this psalm Moses reflected on the brevity of life and the importance of using what time we have left to honor the Lord.

Everlasting God

Psalm 90 begins with Moses' acknowledgment that the Lord's existence spans all generations. Further, Moses identified the Lord as Israel's dwelling place throughout those generations (v. 1). From Abraham to Moses, Israel was a nomadic nation. The people had no permanent city. Although Abraham's grandson Jacob and his family settled in Egypt when Joseph was Egypt's prime minister, their residence was only temporary. After Joseph died, a pharaoh arose who was hostile to the people of Israel. He enslaved them until God liberated them and led them through the wilderness and into Canaan forty years later.

3. Read Hebrews 11:9 and 10. What word would you use to describe Abraham's life in "the land of promise"?

4. What final destination was Abraham anticipating?

5. Read 1 Peter 2:11. What designations did Peter apply to Christians?

6. Why are those designations appropriate?

7. Read 2 Corinthians 5:1. What metaphors did Paul use to refer to the believer's body?

The Lord was Israel's dwelling place (Psalm 90:1), and He is our dwelling place too. He invites us to abide in Him (John 15:4), because we are not of the world (v. 19).

In Psalm 90 Moses next paid tribute to the Lord as the eternal God Who created all things (v. 2). Mountains may look timeless, but they are not. They owe their existence to the Creator, Who is "from everlasting to everlasting."

Finite Man

What a contrast human life is to God's eternal existence! Because we have sinned, we will experience physical death (unless Jesus raptures us in this lifetime). We are turned "to destruction" (Psalm 90:3). Hebrews 9:27 declares, "It is appointed unto men once to die, but after this the judgment." What a grim fact. All of humanity is utterly hopeless without the intervention of God.

8. Write John 3:16 in your own words as you contemplate God's intervention on behalf of mankind.

Although God has given us eternal life, while we live this earthly life, we're constrained by time. To us, a thousand years is a long time. But God considers it merely "as yesterday" and "a watch [four hours] in the night." We are carried along through life as swiftly as a flash flood sweeps up everything in its path. Our time on earth compares to "a sleep." Like grass, we sprout but then are cut down (Psalm 90:4–6).

9. Read Psalm 90:4–6. Which of the metaphors in these verses most clearly communicates the brevity of life to you? Why?

God's Wrath

God's anger and wrath are what cut a person's life short. God takes note of sin—even "secret sins"—and holds accountable those who are not covered by the blood of Christ (vv. 7, 8).

God not only knew the Israelites' sin; He punished them for it. Moses reflected on their wilderness wanderings after they refused to enter Canaan in spite of Joshua and Caleb's assurance that the Canaanites were "bread for us: their defence is departed from them, and the LORD is with us" (Numbers 14:9). "Fear them not," Joshua and Caleb had challenged the nation. The older generation rejected the challenge and, as a consequence, died off in the wilderness. Some reached the age of seventy, and some even reached the age of eighty, but life was difficult for them because of their refusal to take God at His word and invade Canaan (Psalm 90:9–11).

10. What do you see as a few consequences of refusing to take God at His word?

Days in Perspective

That life is brief should motivate us to "number our days" and "apply our hearts unto wisdom" (v. 12). Moses prayed that the Israelites would do so.

11. Number your days by calculating how many days you have already lived and comparing the total to how many days you hope to yet live.

12. What does seeing the actual days you hope to have left in your life do to your urgency to make them count?

Unlike Moses, who predicted the number of years his countrymen might live, we do not know how long we have to live.

13. Read Proverbs 27:1. What cautionary note does this verse raise?

14. What evidence of life's uncertainty have you seen recently?

In his letter "to the twelve tribes which are scattered abroad" (James 1:1), the apostle James taught that life is fleeting. He compared life to a vapor that quickly dissipates (4:14). He urged his readers, therefore, to conduct their daily activities in compliance with God's will (v. 15).

The apostle John affirmed James's counsel. John stressed that the evil world system and its sinful cravings are passing away but that the person who does God's will abides forever (1 John 2:17).

Every believer must choose to obey or disobey God. Whoever chooses to pursue his or her own selfish way will see his or her work disappear in a puff of smoke at the Judgment Seat of Christ, whereas everyone who honors the Lord will receive a reward (1 Corinthians 3:13–15).

15. Read 2 Timothy 4:7 and 8. What lies ahead for believers who finish the course God has planned for them?

A Fresh Start

Moses asked the Lord to turn from His anger and have pity on His people (Psalm 90:13). He wondered how long the Lord would discipline them. He longed for a new day, a fresh start, that would usher in mercy and joy (v. 14). He desired as many days and years of gladness as those that had been filled with the Lord's discipline (v. 15).

16. What will obsessively bemoaning missed opportunities to live for God in the past do to opportunities to live for God today and tomorrow?

Verses 13–15 of Moses' prayer teach us that life can be either burdensome and unhappy or liberating and joyful. The deciding factor is our relationship to the Lord. If we spurn His will, the future will bring regret and dismay; but if we embrace His will, it will bring satisfaction and joy. We may encounter hard trials, but we will enjoy a sense of victory and hope. As the apostle Paul assured us, "the sufferings of this present time are not worthy to be compared with the glory which shall be revealed in us" (Romans 8:18); and he wrote, "We are more than conquerors through him that loved us" (v. 37).

Joshua and Caleb had encouraged the Israelites to sweep into Canaan and claim that fertile land in accordance with God's promises. As a result of their faith and commitment to God's will, they lived to enter and possess Canaan. Meanwhile the bodies of their unbelieving countrymen rotted in the wilderness. Even Moses was barred from entering Canaan because of his disobedient act of smiting the rock at Horeb (Numbers 20:2–13).

God's Favor

Moses longed to see God perform His wondrous works on behalf of Israel and reveal His glory to His people again (Ps. 90:16). He implored God to crown Israel's efforts with favor and grace (v. 17). Our prayers, too, should include a request for a display of God's power in our lives and the gift of His favor and grace on our service for Him. Unless the Lord empowers our service and crowns it with His favor and grace, our work will be in vain. Because life is brief at best and uncertain, we must redeem the time (Ephesians 5:16). Every moment of every day is a precious gift from God to be appreciated and used to honor Him. We cannot count on tomorrow's opportunities. We may not be alive tomorrow. Today is the tomorrow we planned yesterday to devote to the Lord. Now is the only day of opportunity we can seize confidently. Our prayer, like that of Moses, should implore the Lord to crown every effort for Him with favor and grace.

Making It Personal

Time is a precious commodity. We cannot capture yesterday's wasted opportunities, nor can we predict what will happen tomorrow. However, we can learn from past experiences and trust the Lord to bless tomorrow if we live to see it. The wise course of action is to do His will today.

17. As you remember past days or years, what do you regret?

18. As you remember past days or years, what are you most thankful for?

19. If the Lord called you Home today, how confident are you that you have served Him faithfully?

___ not confident   ___ fairly confident   ___ fully confident

20. In light of life's brevity, what three things will you do for the Lord that you have been putting off?

21. Memorize Psalm 90:12.

In the Shadow of the Almighty

God is worthy of a believer's trust.

Psalm 91

"He that dwelleth in the secret place of the most High shall abide under the shadow of the Almighty. I will say of the LORD, He is my refuge and my fortress: my God; in him will I trust" (Psalm 91:1, 2).

A young man was working at a restaurant in Omaha, Nebraska, when he saw something that made his trust in food service employees wane. A cook was making a large pot of corn when he inadvertently dropped his spoon into the pot. Without hesitation the man reached into the pot to retrieve the spoon. His entire hand and a good portion of his hairy arm were submerged in the water while he rummaged for the spoon. When he finally found the spoon and pulled his hand from the pot, he used his other hand to "squeegee" the juice—and who knows what else—from his arm back into the pot.

Many restaurants would go out of business if their customers knew what happened to their food while it was being prepared. Thankfully, for most of us ignorance is bliss. We blindly trust the workers so we can continue to enjoy our eating-out experiences.

When it comes to life and the circumstances you are served, you can accept them with complete trust in the Chef: the Lord. Psalm 91

presents the Lord as trustworthy. Studying the psalm will challenge you
to deepen your trust in God.

Getting Started

1. How much do you know about what goes on in the kitchen of
your favorite restaurant?

2. How much do you want to know about what goes on in your
favorite restaurant's kitchen?

Searching the Scriptures

When we truly see God for Who He is, making a definite decision
to trust Him is not difficult. The first couple of verses of Psalm 91 tell us
important facts about God that form the basis for trust in Him.

God, the Most High

The psalmist's first reference to God is as the "most High" (Psalm
91:1).

3. What comes to your mind when you think of God's being the
"most High"?

4. Read Daniel 4:28–37. What do you learn from Nebuchadnezzar
about God's position as the Most High?

5. What decision did Nebuchadnezzar make when he realized Who God is?

The psalmist described the place of the Most High as "secret" and noted that it is possible for people to at least figuratively dwell there (v. 1). Those who have been privileged to visit a president in his private office have a small sense of the privilege of dwelling in the place of the Most High. The private time spent with someone so powerful must be unforgettable.

The word "secret" refers to a "sheltered or protected hiding place." What makes the place of the Most High so sheltered and protective is the presence of God Himself. Being near the Most High is the securest place a person could ever be. But being near the Most High is not a given. Only those who choose to "dwell" in the secret place of the Most High enjoy the security of His presence.

6. What three words would you use to describe what it means to dwell somewhere?

Dwelling in a place means settling down or remaining with constancy. In essence, choosing to *dwell* in the secret place of the Most High is simply choosing to *trust* the Most High: to rest in Who He is, the highest authority.

Trusting in God is the prerequisite for the promise that the psalmist laid out in the second part of verse 1—a promise that is related to the fact that God is almighty.

God, the Almighty

To be almighty is to be all-powerful. God is almighty, and those who trust in Him will abide in His shadow (v. 1).

7. What does it take to be in someone's shadow?

8. Describe how safe and secure you felt as a child when walking by the side of a trusted adult.

The psalmist clearly said that to choose to trust God is to choose to be next to the Almighty. This is a promise that we can claim today. And what a promise!

God, a Refuge and Fortress

Both a "refuge" and a "fortress" are designed for protection (v. 2). Those who run to them find security. The psalmist called the Lord his refuge and fortress. In this way he was taking the idea of dwelling in the shadow of the Lord a step further. He saw himself as not just next to the Lord but as dwelling *in* the Lord.

9. Read 2 Samuel 22:1–7. What did it take for David to "enter" his refuge, the Lord?

10. What other "fortresses" might believers try to run to when they face turmoil?

After stating in Psalm 91:2 God's ultimate position, almighty power, and absolute protection, the psalmist simply stated that the Lord was his God and that he would trust in Him. God didn't make the psalmist just *feel* safe and secure; He actually *made* him safe and secure.

Feelings should not dictate decisions; they should follow decisions. When David was fleeing Saul, he felt alone, abandoned, and hopeless (2 Samuel 22:7). But he chose to trust in the Lord. His choice to trust made him safe, and his feelings of safety followed.

The psalmist could have stopped with verses 1 and 2. His mind was made up. He had chosen to trust the Most High and Almighty God. But he continued with the rest of his song to encourage others to trust in the Lord too.

God, the Caregiver

The "snare" referred to in Psalm 91:3 was the trap set by a "fowler," or bird catcher. Ancient fowlers were particularly cunning. They often took the young of the birds they hunted and raised them until they were tame. Then they put the tame birds in cages and used their calls to attract other birds. When a flock was gathered, the fowler used a net, arrows, or a throwing stick to capture or kill the birds. Even a surprise attack like that of a fowler cannot trap those who trust in the Lord.

11. Read Proverbs 29:25. What does this proverb say about what protects a person from a snare?

God also promises to deliver from the "pestilence," or plague, those who trust Him (Psalm 91:3). Plagues are devastating and seem to run through a population as if they were alive, arbitrarily choosing whom they will inflict. Even today with our superior medical knowledge, plagues threaten us. We cannot absolutely control their spread and harmful effects. But God can. The psalmist was pointing out that God can control that which baffles mankind. In the midst of terrifying uncertainty like that caused by a rampant plague, God can be trusted.

12. Read Psalm 91:4. What two words would you use to describe God on the basis of the metaphors in this verse?

The flimsy wing of a bird doesn't seem like a place of protection. After all, a bird's wing is not exactly impenetrable. However, the psalmist was trying to convey care more than protection. God cares for those who are His much like a mother bird cares for her young.

By contrast, a "shield and buckler" are strong and offer secure protection (v. 4). When used by an Old Testament soldier, the shield received the brunt of an enemy's blows. When we think of God as our shield, we become aware of the grief we are spared as we trust Him to direct us with His truth.

13. Read Ephesians 6:16. What is the relationship between protection and faith, or trust, in this verse?

God, the Giver of Peace

14. Read Psalm 91:5 and 6. What factor does darkness play in heightening your fears?

The terror of the night is being unable to see the enemy. The terror of the day is that the enemy can see us. In other words, there is no rest for the hunted. But God takes away both fears. Addressing those who feel that they cannot escape and find rest for their souls, the psalmist encouraged trust in the Almighty and Most High God. His presence in the midst of uncertainty chases away fear and gives peace (Philippians 4:6, 7).

15. Describe a time when you were relieved of dreadful fear and anxiety by simply praying about the matter and expressing your trust in the Lord.

The wicked will not go unpunished. They will get their "reward" (Psalm 91:8). Though in this life some of the wicked may appear to be happy, content, and full, their day is coming. They will not be able to escape the wrath of God.

God, Your Assurance of Safety

The psalmist's solicitation to trust in the Lord is convincing—so much so that the writer expected the reader to choose to trust God. He didn't say in verse 9, "If perchance you have now chosen to trust God." No, he said, "Because thou hast made the LORD, which is my refuge, even the most High, thy habitation."

Having already laid out the benefits of trusting God in verses 3–8, the psalmist simply summarized them and applied them to the reader personally (v. 10).

God uses angels to ensure the safety of His own. He gives the angels a "charge" (v. 11). In other words, He tells them what to do, and they carry out His will in regard to believers. In a general sense the angels are sent to "keep," or protect, believers.

16. Read Hebrews 1:14. Describe instances when you sensed God's protection through His angels.

Angels make a difference in our lives. Psalm 91:12 tells us that they intervene and keep us from harm. A credit card company recently used people dressed like angels in their television ads. The angels were less than adequate. Instead of helping the people they were supposed to be watching, they allowed themselves to be distracted. One angel let a guy go swimming in shark-infested waters while he was busy doing something else. Of course when it came time to choose a credit card, the angel was right there to help the person make the right decision. Real angels aren't so sporadic in carrying out their duties. They are all well-equipped to do their jobs. God trusts them, and we can find comfort in knowing they are near.

God also gives believers strength for the way (v. 13). Treading on a lion and a cobra is unordinary. Paul knew such unordinary strength. He said, "I can do all things through Christ which strengtheneth me" (Philippians 4:13). God strengthens us to meet the challenges of life as we trust Him and choose to obey Him.

God, the Promise Maker

Psalm 91:14–16 records what God Himself said to the psalmist about those who have put their trust in God. His words include some precious promises.

The first and last phrases in verse 14 could be used interchangeably. Loving God is equivalent to knowing and trusting God's name (the Most High and Almighty, v. 1). As believers think about the psalmist's statement of trust, look at the reasons for trusting God, and then decide to trust God (v. 9), they are also choosing to love God.

17. How can you get to know God's name better?

In response to the love of believers, the Lord promises to deliver them and lift them up on high, where they will be safe. Though the trouble still exists, they can know that God is in control and that they can endure with peace and assurance.

Furthermore, God declares to those who trust Him that He will listen to them if they will but call on Him.

18. Read Psalm 91:15. How should the promises of God in verse 15 affect your prayer life?

God also promises His presence in the midst of trouble. Psalm 91:15 says, "I will be with him in trouble." Notice that this verse does not say, "I will take the trouble away." But it does teach that God's presence in the trouble is just as good as being out of trouble.

A long life is also promised to all those who place their trust in God. Someone may protest that a number of the most devoted of souls have lived relatively short lives. But when we take into consideration that the days they did live were satisfying and that since their deaths, their satisfaction has continued in God's presence, we can know that God has never reneged on His promise. Those who choose to trust in

God and live for Him will find a satisfaction in this life that will continue forever in eternity, where they will ultimately realize God's salvation (v. 16).

Making It Personal

19. a. Finish the following phrase: My life would be a lot better if . . . *(e.g., I didn't have cancer; my job wasn't so difficult).*

b. Now read the following ending: My life would be a lot better if *I learned to trust God more.* Don't spend your life trying to control circumstances and avoid trouble. Rather, commit to trusting God. He is worthy of your trust!

20. Memorize Psalm 91:1 and 2.

Dependent Parents

*Parents must depend on God
in raising their children.*

Psalm 127

"Lo, children are an heritage of the LORD: and the fruit of the womb is his reward. As arrows are in the hand of a mighty man; so are children of the youth. Happy is the man that hath his quiver full of them: they shall not be ashamed, but they shall speak with the enemies in the gate" (Psalm 127:3–5).

Supernanny, we need your help!" So say the seemingly endless string of parents who appear on the television show *Supernanny.* The kids on the show who are screaming, hitting, and sometimes even spitting at their parents are obviously out of control. So Supernanny shows up, trains the parents in parenting techniques, and turns the chaotic family into a civilized family.

Supernanny is widely popular, and she seems to have some tried and true techniques for parenting. But when watching the show, one cannot help but realize that something or Someone is missing. Psalm 127 provides parents with answers that go beyond modifying children's behavior to shaping their hearts.

Getting Started

1. To what do you attribute the success of *Supernanny?*

2. How do you explain the seemingly successful outcomes on this show?

Searching the Scriptures

As believers, we have Someone far greater than a super nanny to help us in raising children—we have the Creator Himself as our guide. This study of Psalm 127 will look at the folly of parenting without God's help and the blessings of depending on Him.

Overplanning Parents

3. Read the first half of Psalm 127:1. What might the psalmist have meant by the phrase "build the house"?

In Psalm 127:1, the psalmist, either Solomon or David, is primarily referring to constructing a building. But the principle of verse 1 is that all human effort is vain without God's help. The verse even states that *God* is doing the building and implies that the human builders are His helpers. The principle of this verse can be applied to building a family.

4. What must a builder do before he or she can successfully construct a building?

Unless builders have plans, they will not know what to do. But just having a plan is not enough. Builders must have the right plan.

Many parents devise their own plans for raising their children. One such plan is to dictate every little thing their children will do. They hope that their controlling their children's actions and activities will make their children good. Their plan, in essence, is to keep their children doing good things so they don't have time to get into trouble.

5. What are some plans that parents might lay out for their children to divert them from getting into trouble?

6. Why doesn't simply planning a lot of activity to keep a child out of trouble make that child godly?

7. What, or Who, is missing from the overplanning parent's approach to raising children? (See Psalm 127:1.)

The overplanning parents' efforts are "vain." They will never work. They are as empty as the wind, for they never address the needs of the child's heart.

Children who are raised by overplanning parents will often be good kids until they move away from home. They then display the lack of spiritual moorings in their lives—the moorings that busyness failed to develop in them.

Instead of being overplanning parents, moms and dads need to turn to the Lord. He has a plan for all His children that goes much deeper than just being busy and staying out of trouble.

8. What are some of God's plans for children—plans that parents need to adopt as their own? (See Galatians 5:22–26, Ephesians 4:17–32 and 6:1–3, and Philippians 2:1–5.)

9. When parents surrender the planning of their children's lives, what does it look like practically?

Overprotective Parents

The second self-reliant approach to parenting is overprotection. This type of parenting can also be called helicopter parenting because the parents hover over their children constantly. The goal of helicopter parents is to protect their children from any bad influences and to directly influence nearly every decision they make.

10. Read Psalm 127:1. How might the picture of the watchman and the city relate to overprotective parenting?

We live in an evil world, and the threats to our children from their peers, the Internet, television, and music are real. Parents do indeed have the responsibility to shield their children from these corrupt influences. But parents should not count on themselves as the sole watchmen for their children. The job is too big and utterly impossible. There are always opportunities for the enemy to slip by.

11. What are some opportunities Satan might have to slip by the watchful eyes of a parent?

A father observed his young boy coming out of the bathroom in his home and realized his son had not washed his hands. The father reminded the son to wash his hands as he had been told countless times before. The son obediently returned to the bathroom to do as he was told. He then revealed to his dad that when he is alone, he just sneaks out of the bathroom without washing his hands. The son's glib confession opened his father's eyes. The son was willing to obey when Dad was watching but not when Dad was absent. In response, the father sat his son down and reinforced in him an awareness of God's presence and the impossibility of sneaking disobediently away from God.

Children cannot be controlled by the presence of their parents, because their parents simply cannot be with them every moment of every day. And even if they were, a parent can be completely unaware of the rebellion and disobedience going on inside his or her child's heart. A child's obedience will ultimately come in response to an awareness of God's presence and the responsibility to obey Him through His enabling power.

12. How can parents build into their children a sense of God's watchfulness? (See Psalm 139:1–18, Proverbs 4, Ephesians 6:4, and Hebrew 4:12 and 13.)

Overworking Parents

Overworking is the final self-reliant approach to parenting addressed by the principles in Psalm 127. Verse 2 states the vanity of extending the workday by getting up early and staying up late. The term "bread of sorrows" refers to experiencing the toil of labor. This verse is not encouraging laziness; rather it is discouraging the practice of fretting and working unnecessarily long hours to secure more money.

Often the intent of the overworking parent is to earn enough money to buy the happiness and loyalty of the child.

13. a. What do children typically want more: the stuff their parents buy for them or their parents' time and attention?

b. Why is this so?

God offers sleep to those who feel frazzled by the frantic pace they have chosen if they will stop relying on themselves (v. 2). Rest comes from God as we are rightly related to Him, not as we amass more money and possessions.

14. Read Matthew 8:23–26. What is true of the person who is able to sleep well?

A parent will never be able to buy his or her child's loyalty and happiness. Working hard is commendable, but not when it supplants a parent's trust in the Lord.

As has been clearly established, parenting done through self-reliance is vain. Conversely, parenting done by relying on God is profitable and ultimately successful.

God-Given Children

Children are from the Lord; they are a heritage, or an inheritance, from God (Psalm 127:3). Knowing that our children come from God should give us a measure of comfort.

15. Read Psalm 127:3. What are the implications of the truth that children are a heritage from the Lord?

Relying on God for direction and the strength to teach our children in the way they should go makes perfect sense, since our children are from God and He cares for them deeply.

Children are also a "reward" (v. 3). They are a benefit to their parents. Seeing all children as a reward is not the prevailing viewpoint in society today.

16. What criteria must often be met before a child is considered a "reward" by society today?

Not every parent is prepared to raise a child. In these instances, giving a child up for adoption is a God-honoring step to take. Such an action recognizes the value of the child and the need for the child to receive necessary care and attention.

God-Shaped Children

The psalmist went on to state that children are like arrows "in the hand of a mighty man" (v. 4).

17. Read Psalm 127:4.

    a. How are children like arrows?

    b. What does it take to make arrows?

God shapes children and prepares them to take flight. He whittles them until they are straight and ready for His use. This process starts as soon as a baby is born and continues until the child leaves home. But parents can get in the way of God's purposes for their children. They can try to shape and bend their little arrows to fulfill their own desires.

18. What goals might parents set for their children that could interfere with God's goals for them?

Parents who depend on God will seek God's will for their children. They will depend on Him to mold and shape their children so they are ready for what He wants them to do not only as adults but also as they are growing up.

Our dependence on God as we raise the children He has entrusted to us will make a difference in eternity—not just for our children, but for the lives they touch as they live for the Lord. God has big plans for our children if we will but surrender our children to Him and let Him shape their lives.

God-blessed Children

The children who are shaped by God because their parents relied on Him will be successful in life. These children won't be ashamed of their lives (v. 5). They won't regret having followed the Lord. They will be victorious.

To "speak with the enemies in the gate" meant that the children would represent the family well in the place where disputes were often settled. The principle is that the children will be ready for life and will live it in a manner that represents the family and the Lord well. The children described in verse 5 are functioning well because their parents followed God's plan for their children's lives, instilled in their children a sense of God's presence, and taught them to seek God rather than money and possessions.

19. Who deserves the ultimate praise for children who grow up to be winners?

It is important to remember that while parents certainly have a responsibility to raise their children according to God's ways, no parent can know how his or her children will ultimately respond to God. Every child is responsible for his or her own life. No child, no matter how corrupt the parents were, can excuse rebellious living by blaming inadequate parents.

Success in parenting is not measured by how well the children turn out. Success is measured by the opportunity the parents provided for their children to know and do God's will.

Making It Personal

All parents are inadequate. That is the main point of Psalm 127. This means all parents need to seek forgiveness from God for the ways they have failed and to renew their dependence on God for the future.

20. What will happen to parents' effectiveness if they continuously feel guilty for how they raised, or are raising, their children?

21. Take your failures and sins as a parent to God and rest in His forgiveness. Write a short prayer praising God for His complete forgiveness.

22. How can you deepen your dependence on God as a parent?

23. If you are not a parent, write a prayer asking God to help you be an example to the children you know and minister to.

24. Memorize Psalm 127:3–5.

Worship from the Heart

God's character and ways are worthy to be praised.

Psalm 138

"I will praise thee with my whole heart: before the gods will I sing praise unto thee. I will worship toward thy holy temple, and praise thy name for thy lovingkindness and for thy truth: for thou hast magnified thy word above all thy name" (Psalm 138:1, 2).

Everybody is an expert in something. For you it might be cooking, furniture refinishing, carpet laying, gardening, raising children, or interior decorating. Whatever your expertise, you most likely were not born an expert. You had to invest time in learning your skill before you could call yourself an expert.

Getting Started

1. What are you an expert in? What did it take to become an expert in the area you named?

2. How does someone become an expert in God?

3. How should knowing God well affect our lives?

Searching the Scriptures

The first three verses of Psalm 138 are in essence David's testimony about praising God. David was devoted to praising God and did not see it as a once-a-week task or as an optional activity. Praising and worshiping God were a vital part of his life. All believers can emulate David's devotion to praising God even though they may feel comfortable singing only in the shower. Musical talent is not a prerequisite for praising God.

David Praised God from the Heart

David began his psalm of praise to God by stating that he was praising God with his "whole heart" (v. 1).

4. Read Psalm 138:1. What does it mean to praise God with your "whole heart"?

5. How do you feel when someone pays you a compliment when that person really doesn't mean it?

6. How do you think God responds to halfhearted praise? (See Isaiah 29:13 and 14.)

A car dealer's praise of a Dodge Grand Caravan is meaningless if he chooses to drive a Toyota Sienna himself. Similarly, our praise of God is not genuine if we are actually worshiping someone or something besides God. Though we might sing with the full capacity of our lungs, God will listen only if we are also singing with the full capacity of our hearts. God isn't impressed with sound, just with the source of the sound.

David Praised God before All People

David said he would wholeheartedly worship God "before the gods" (Psalm 138:1). On the surface it seems David was communicating that other gods do indeed exist. But he was not trying to convey that idea. David was simply saying that he was uninhibited in his worship of God. He praised Him even in the face of other gods—the unlikeliest of audiences had they actually existed.

7. How might a believer today demonstrate to the lost that he or she wholeheartedly praises God?

8. Evaluate this statement: I don't want to offend my unbelieving friends, so I keep my worship of God to myself.

Believers who think that praising God is something they need do only on Sundays are mistaken. Worshiping God is a way of life. We ought to exude worship of God. Our neighbors, coworkers, and friends should clearly know that we worship the Lord.

David Praised God's Absolute Holiness

David's devotion to praising and worshiping God was grounded in his understanding of God's character.

David directed his worship of God toward God's "holy temple" (v. 2). Since the first temple was not built until Solomon was on the throne, David was most likely referring to the tabernacle. The tabernacle was seen as God's dwelling place. It was where man and God met. God's presence in the tabernacle made the tabernacle "holy."

9. Read Leviticus 10:1–3 and 16:1 and 2. Under the Mosaic law, how important was recognizing the holiness of God's presence in the tabernacle?

David recognized the absolute purity and holiness of God in comparison to sinful mankind. This recognition caused him to worship God.

10. Read Isaiah 6:1–5. How did Isaiah respond when he understood the holiness of God?

Today we must not be lax in recognizing the holiness of God. It is God's holiness that primarily separates God from all else. No one is like God in His absolute purity and perfection. Yet His holiness forms the standard for our lives (1 Peter 1:13–16). All we do, say, or think is to be measured against the holiness of God. We must praise Him for it.

God no longer dwells in a tabernacle or in a temple. He now dwells in our hearts, and we have immediate access to Him. His nearness ought to drive us to worship Him and to do so from a clean heart.

David Praised God's Loving-kindness and Truth

The psalmist connected loving-kindness and truth and gave them as the next reason he decided to sing praise to God (Psalm 138:2). The important connection between loving-kindness and truth should not be overlooked.

11. What would God be like if He were loving but not true?

12. What would God be like if He were true but not loving?

David pointed to both God's loving-kindness and His truth as vital to God's covenant with him and his descendants (2 Samuel 7:10–29). Psalm 89:30–37 makes David's personal dependence on God's loving-kindness and truth very clear.

13. Read Psalm 89:30–37. Why are God's loving-kindness and truth so important in your life, particularly as you claim God's promises?

David Praised God for His Everlasting Word

The last phrase in Psalm 138:2 can be rendered, "God has magnified His word and name above all else." Christ said, "Heaven and earth shall pass away, but my words shall not pass away" (Matthew 24:35). No object will stand the test of time as God's Word will. This truth was comforting to David. He could peer into the future and know that God's word would be the same forever because God is the same forever (Psalm 102:25–28; Isaiah 51:6).

14. What would your life as a believer be like if you had no guarantees that God's words would last forever?

Knowing God's word would last forever caused David to praise God. We, too, ought to praise God for His everlasting words.

David Praised God's Emboldening Strength

David had a multitude of opportunities to see God prove Himself. Without fail, God always came through for David (Psalm 138:3). Notice that David didn't say that God took all his problems away when he cried out to Him. Instead God gave David what he needed to endure the difficulties he faced. God made him bold and gave him an inner strength. The apostle Paul knew such strength (2 Corinthians 12:9).

If we could go back in time and spend a day with David while he was on the run from Saul, we would appreciate the strength God gave to him (1 Samuel 23:14–16). That strength caused David to praise God (Psalm 52:8, 9; Psalm 54).

15. Read 1 Samuel 23:19–29. How would the average person feel while being chased down by Saul?

16. Read Psalm 54. Describe how David actually felt about God while running from Saul.

We can look back over our lives and see times when God's strength emboldened us and carried us through difficult times. For such help we ought to praise the Lord.

Kings of the Earth Praise God

David was not only an excellent example of praise, he also looked forward to the day when all the kings of the earth will praise the Lord (Psalm 138:4). In the Millennium all the kings of the earth will praise God's words. At that time Jesus will be ruling the world from His throne in Jerusalem.

17. Read Isaiah 11:9 and 10. Compare the nations' response to Jesus in the Millennium to their response to Him right now.

The thought of all the kings of the earth uniting in chorus to God is hard to imagine. But one day it will happen. The kings of the earth will then know what we already know today: God's words are praiseworthy (Psalm 119:103, 105, 130, 160).

In the Millennium the kings of the earth will also exalt God for His glorious ways (138:5). When we think of Jesus as high and lifted up in the Millennium and all the nations of the world praising Him, He almost seems inaccessible, particularly to the lowly. But David defeated such a notion with the truths of verse 6: "Though the LORD be high, yet hath he respect unto the lowly." God regards the lowly, or humble, in this world. That is the essence of His ways.

18. Read James 4:4–10. What does this passage say about the ways of God?

19. Read Psalm 138:6. How successful will the person be who proudly tries to impress God with how good or hardworking he or she is?

We have a clearer picture than David did of what will happen in the future. If David praised God for what was yet to happen, we ought to resound with even louder praise. We can praise God both for His future dominion and for His words and ways today.

David Praised God's Protecting Hand

David had full confidence in God's protecting hand. He praised God for what He had done for David in the past (v. 3), and he had no reason to doubt that God's hand would be diligent, enhancing, and trustworthy (v. 7).

20. Read Psalm 138:7. What did David imply when he said that God would "revive" him?

David faced threats, discouragement, and fears, but he knew that God would carry him through them all and revive, or sustain, him (cf. 2 Corinthians 4:7–15).

When our circumstances are out of our hands, we can be assured that they are not out of God's hands. Even the circumstances that ultimately lead to our death are in God's hands, and we can praise and trust Him through them all. Job had such a confidence in God that he said he would trust God even if God slew him (Job 13:15).

When we walk in the "midst of trouble" (Psalm 138:7), we can be confident in God. Even in the face of death we can confidently praise God and trust in Him.

David Praised God's Perfecting Hand

The psalmist believed that God would "perfect," or complete, that which concerned him (v. 8). He had an enduring faith that God's plan would not fail. God had made a covenant with David, and he knew that God would never break His promises to him.

Believers today can exercise the same faith in God. Philippians 1:6 tells us that we can have confidence that God will never stop working in our hearts and lives. We are the work of His hands, and He desires to shape us more and more each day into a perfect reflection of His Son (Ephesians 2:10). God's work and our transformation is possible because God is merciful.

21. Read Psalm 138:8. If God's mercy had an expiration date, how would that limitation affect your future?

David ended his psalm of praise to God with a simple request: "Forsake not the works of thine own hands" (v. 8). God wants to hear our requests. David began with praise to God, but he never presumed upon God. His praise was followed by supplication—asking God to do what He already had promised He would.

Our praise of God must be coupled with our supplication. If we only tell God how wonderful He is but never ask Him to work in our lives, our words are empty. The highest compliment we can give God is to ask for His help. When our requests land on God's ears, He hears them as praise.

Making It Personal

Often we don't praise God because we have a clouded or incomplete view of Who He really is. We must actively seek to get to know God. Our response then should be one of praise.

22. How actively have you sought to learn about both God's character and His ways?

23. As you read your Bible, look for descriptions and illustrations of God's character and ways. Keep a running list in a notebook of what you learn about God from your Bible reading. Review your list often and use it to foster praise to God. First Samuel 17, Psalm 145, and John 6:1–21 are all good places to start this exercise.

Remember that God often reveals Himself most understandably in the accounts of the Bible. As you read them, don't forget that God is the main character. Always ask yourself, What does this story reveal to me about God?

24. Memorize Psalm 138:1 and 2.

Lesson 12

Responding to an Infinite God

God's attributes demand believers' obedience.

Psalm 139

"How precious also are thy thoughts unto me, O God! how great is the sum of them! If I should count them, they are more in number than the sand: when I awake, I am still with thee" (Psalm 139:17, 18).

For parents, sometimes ignorance is bliss—particularly when it comes to their children's crazy stunts. Most people grow up without telling their parents all that they did as children. Things like jumping from a garage roof onto a trampoline or sneaking out of the house for a midnight swim are often not disclosed to parents until years later.

Unlike parents, God cannot be fooled. No one acts outside God's full awareness. He knows all and is everywhere at all times.

Getting Started

1. Name something you did as a child that you didn't tell your parents about for a long time.

2. How did the presence of your parents affect your behavior?

David began Psalm 139 with a testimony of God's absolute knowledge of him. He said that God had "searched" him and "known" him (v. 1). The idea of the word "searched" is like the effort that a thief puts into a burglary. He searches every nook and cranny of the place he is burglarizing—even the places that would normally not contain valuables.

3. Think as a thief thinks. If you were to burglarize a house, what are some unlikely places in the house you might look for valuables?

People used to put their money or jewelry in their freezers because thieves didn't think to look there for valuables. After years of such a practice, thieves have caught on. The freezer is no longer a safe place for valuables.

We can't hide anything from God, for He knows us better than we know ourselves. He has a perfect knowledge of us.

God Knows Our Actions

We often think we know what we have done with our lives until we try to remember what happened just a few years ago or even just a few days ago.

4. What were you specifically doing five years ago at this exact same time?

What about five days ago at this exact time?

What about yesterday at this exact time?

Undoubtedly—unless you were getting married or giving birth, or unless some other dramatic or traumatic event was taking place—you have to admit that you don't have a clue about what you did five years ago, possibly five days ago, or sometimes even what you did a day ago. It is somewhat disturbing to realize that we forget the majority of our actions.

5. Read the first half of verses 2 and 3 of Psalm 139. How well is God acquainted with our actions?

The first part of verse 2 is constructed as a merism. A merism is a figure of speech that identifies contrasting parts as a means of referring to the whole. So when David listed his "downsitting" and "uprising," he was referring to all the actions he did between sitting down and getting up.

In verse 3 David listed his "path" and his "lying down" as within God's knowledge. This is another merism. David's public path and his private lying down and everything that happened in between were known by God. The word "compassest" in verse 3 refers to winnowing or scattering. The idea is that nothing is hidden from God. He clearly sees all of our actions. God is "acquainted" with all our ways (v. 3).

God never forgets even our smallest good deeds. He remembers when we open a door for someone or make a meal for a friend in need.

6. What are some of the most inconsequential good deeds you have done for someone recently?

7. How important did you think they were when you did them?

God's memories of our actions make them valuable. At the Judgment Seat of Christ we will receive rewards for our service for the Lord—no matter how inconsequential they seemed (2 Corinthians 5:10).

God Knows Our Thoughts

God's knowledge of us runs deeper than our actions. God also knows our thoughts.

8. Read the second half of Psalm 139:2. What is your immediate reaction to hearing this verse?

God knew David's thoughts "afar off." This is perhaps a reference to time rather than distance. David most likely meant that God knew all of his past and future thoughts.

"Thought" includes our motivations and attitudes. God knows why we do what we do. He peers right into our hearts. He knows when we are doing something to please ourselves or to make ourselves look good.

God Knows Our Words

Often we will say, "I knew you were going to say that," to someone we know well. Parents often become predictable in their responses to their children—especially as their children get older.

9. What predictable responses did your parents give you as you were growing up?

10. Read Psalm 139:4. Was David simply saying that God was acquainted with his speech patterns and his typical responses? Explain.

The idea of verse 4 goes beyond just learning how a person typically responds to situations. God knows our words before we ever utter them. In this sense God could say, "I knew you were going to say that," after every word we say.

God Knows Us Completely

David ended his section on God's knowledge as he had begun it—with a broad statement on how much God knew about him. He said that God had "beset" him "behind and before" (v. 5). The idea is that God had enclosed him or hedged him in. In other words, David had no means of escape. David knew that God had always and would always know every single thing about him.

It is impossible to comprehend all the information that God simultaneously processes every single moment of time. His knowledge is absolutely amazing. That is why David said, "Such knowledge is too wonderful for me; it is high, I cannot attain unto it" (v. 6). "Wonderful" means "surpassing" or "extraordinary."

11. Contemplate God's omniscience. What are some of the minutest details that God knows?

When we try to think of God's omniscience, we have to conclude with David that such a thought is beyond our comprehension.

We Cannot Run or Hide from God

For those who don't like God's knowing all there is to know about them, trying to run or hide from God seems like the logical action to take. David showed the futility of such a response with his description of God's omnipresence in verses 7–12.

David began his section on God's omnipresence with a couple of rhetorical questions to underscore the futility of trying to run from God (v. 7).

12. Read Psalm 139:7. What are some examples of Biblical characters who tried to run from God? How successful were they?

David used another merism in verse 8. Heaven and Hell, the highest and lowest of all places, are used to convey that God is everywhere. Even the deepest part of the sea, the Marianas Trench—a place where man had not been until 1951—is graced with the presence of God. Running from God is a hopeless endeavor.

Jonah is the classic example of the futility of trying to run from God. God ran along with him and would not leave his side. When Jonah told the sailors to throw him into the sea to stop the storm, he must have thought that God wouldn't follow him into the sea. But God was with him. Swallowed by a fish, Jonah found nowhere else to run. It was then that he remembered God (Jonah 2). God heard his cry and delivered him (vv. 2, 10).

Those who try to run from God are, in the end, often glad that they could not get away, for God is the only One Who can pick them up again. Like Jonah, they can say, "Yet hast thou brought up my life from corruption, O LORD my God" (v. 6). They know firsthand the truth of Psalm 139:10.

13. Read Psalm 139:10. When, if ever, have you tried to run from God?

14. How did God let you know that He was still with you and ready to lead you?

Though played for generations, hide-and-seek is still a favorite children's game. Often the darker the hiding places, the better. Those who try to hide from God also seek a proverbial darkness (v. 11). They want to be invisible to God. But God's night vision is so good that the night is like day to the Lord (v. 12). There is no such thing as a darkness that hides anything from God's eyes.

15. Why might people want to hide from the Lord?

Those who realize that trying to escape God's knowledge of them by fleeing from Him is pointless might then conclude that they can still have power over their own lives. Again David showed the futility of such a thought with his description of God's omnipotence in verses 13–18.

God's Creative and Sovereign Power

The greatest power that exists is the power to create life. God, as the creator of all life, is the possessor of the greatest power of all. David acknowledged that God was his Creator and therefore had power over him.

The first part of verse 13 refers to the creation of David's heart ("reins"), or his innermost being. The second part of the verse refers to the creation of David's body in his mother's womb. "Covered" could be rendered "wove." God's power is active in weaving each person's body and in creating each person's heart.

Knowing that he was a direct result of God's handiwork, David responded by praising God (v. 14). He took a look at his body and realized that it would not work without the superintending hand of God. David was convinced of such a conclusion. When David wrote, "And that my soul knoweth right well," he was stating the firmness of his belief that God was his Creator.

We know far more than David did, but our knowledge is still only a fraction of what could be known about the human body. We—more than all who have lived before us—ought to praise our Creator.

In verse 15 David added that God wasn't oblivious to the formation of his bones ("substance") even though at that time the womb was as hidden as "the lowest parts of the earth." Today, images of babies as they form in their mothers' wombs are easily accessible through ultrasounds. But the actual forming of the body is still completely up to God. Science has never and will never be able to create life. That power will always belong to God.

16. Why is recognizing God as the Creator of our bodies so important?

Not only is God our Creator, but He also is our sovereign planner. The phrase "which in continuance where fashioned" is a reference to laying out the details of David's days before he was even born (v. 16). When David thought of the interest that God had in him and his life, he was grateful.

17. Read Psalm 139:17 and 18. If God were to send you a thinking-of-you card today, what would the card say?

The Appropriate Responses to God

David had many enemies, and some of them were bloodthirsty men (v. 19). He trusted God to deal properly with his enemies, for they were also God's enemies (v. 20). David expressed his hatred for those who hated his God (v. 21), and he considered any enemy of God his enemy (v. 22).

David couldn't handle his enemies on his own. He trusted God to help him. Most believers today are probably not personally running from bloodthirsty men. But we are facing situations that make us feel helpless.

18. What situations can make a person feel helpless?

19. How should the truths about God in Psalm 139:1–18 affect the helpless-feeling believer?

David chose to be loyal to God because he believed that God is all-knowing, everywhere-present, and all-powerful. David was even willing to put his loyalty to God to the ultimate test—God's searching eyes (vv. 23, 24). After studying Psalm 139, we also ought to respond to God with trust and deep loyalty.

Making It Personal

20. What helpless situations are you currently facing?

21. What differences will the truths of Psalm 139 make in your life?

22. Marvel at Who God is and praise Him for the help He will bring your way.

23. Memorize Psalm 139:17 and 18.

Good Singing!

Singing praises to God is good and beautiful.

Psalm 147

"Praise ye the LORD: for it is good to sing praises unto our God; for it is pleasant; and praise is comely" (Psalm 147:1).

Ever get to praising God and inadvertently break into song? Ever sing a few bars before realizing someone is giving you a what-is-that-racket look? What did you do? Most likely you stopped singing because it suddenly felt awkward and out of place. Your praise stopped when your self-consciousness kicked in.

Have you ever thought about what God thinks when you abruptly stop singing to Him? Unless you have a great singing voice, you might imagine He would say something like, "Thank you. That was nice, but please don't ever do that again." In reality God loves to hear all praises that are sung to Him—no matter the quality of the voice. He must be disappointed when we stop our singing because we are too embarrassed to continue.

God gave people like David a tremendous ability to sing. But that doesn't mean we should leave singing to the professionals. God wants all of us to sing to Him. Psalm 147 communicates God's desire for us to sing praises to His name.

Getting Started

1. Where do you tend to do most of your singing?

2. What are some of your favorite songs of praise to God?

3. If you could write a song of praise to God, what about God would you include in your song?

Searching the Scriptures

God's Desire to Hear Songs

After reading this lesson up to this point, you might be thinking that singing is not for you, so the rest of this lesson isn't going to mean much. The writer of Psalm 147 would disagree. He not only encouraged us to sing to the Lord, but he also commanded it (v. 7). Furthermore, he began the psalm with some reasons why singing to the Lord is appropriate for all.

4. Read Psalm 147:1. What three reasons did the psalmist give for singing to the Lord?

You may not be a good singer; but your singing, when it is directed to God, is "good." It is right, fitting, and beneficial. There is nothing wrong with it, and it will do you good. So go ahead and sing. God has given you the green light no matter what your singing voice is like!

5. In what ways is praising God "good" for a believer? Consider the sins that praising God helps a believer to avoid.

Praise is also "pleasant." God delights in praise. He becomes excited when He hears your personal words of praise. His infiniteness allows Him to give His full attention to the words of your song. It's as if He is sitting and listening to a private concert by you. And He thoroughly enjoys your concert every time.

6. How should the image of you giving God a private concert affect your praise to God?

Third, praise is beautiful ("comely"). Have you ever said, "That was beautiful" after hearing a song? That is the idea being conveyed by the psalmist. To God, all praise is like hearing a beautiful song. How encouraging to know that God enjoys our songs of praise and says, "That was beautiful" every time we finish singing.

God's Care

Verses 2–6 begin a long list of reasons to praise God that extends to the end of the psalm. The list needs to be seen as a short list. The psalm would go on and on if every reason to praise God were listed. As it is, we have plenty to think about in the psalm and to keep us busy praising God.

The psalmist began his list by stating that the Lord builds up Jerusalem. Ever since David ascended to the throne of Israel, Jerusalem has been the focal city for the Jews. After the Exile, God sent leaders such as Ezra, Zerubbabel, and Nehemiah to rebuild Jerusalem both spiritually and structurally. During those years a remnant of the scattered Jews returned to the city and once again dwelt in the land.

In the Millennium God will again build Jerusalem and establish the city as the focal point in the world. God's dealings with the Jews demonstrates His care and concern for outcasts as well as His grace and mercy to mankind.

Verse 3 describes God's care for the brokenhearted. God is not like the type of doctor who fixes patients' bodies but could care less about the troubles they are going through. God binds up their "wounds." "Wounds" is a reference to "grief." God helps those whose hearts are troubled.

7. When have you had a doctor who really cared about you? What difference did his or her concern make in your life?

The psalmist moved from the depths of the hurting heart in verse 3 to the ends of the universe in verse 4. This abrupt change of subject might seem out of place. But God's care for the stars that no one can even see says a lot about His character. If God is interested in the stars and has even taken the time to name them all, then His care for people must be even greater.

Verse 5 shifts the subject again. This time the focus is on God's power and understanding. The great power and infinite understanding of God might cause us to think of Him as unapproachable and aloft. But it is actually both God's great power and His unlimited understanding that should give us personal comfort. There is nothing that God is powerless to do for His own, and there is nothing about us that He doesn't understand.

8. How likely are we to praise God if we are continually focused on what frustrates and irritates us?

The focus in verse 6 comes back down to earth and settles on the "meek" and humble. The humble recognize God as mighty in power and infinite in understanding. For such recognition, God lifts them up.

The wicked, on the other hand, refuse to submit to God. For this, God will cast them down to the ground.

God's Deeds

The psalmist interrupted his list of reasons to praise God with a couple of commands. The first command is to "sing unto the LORD with thanksgiving" (v. 7). The word for "sing" in this verse connotes singing that comes as a response. So we are to respond to the Lord with a song of thanks. Verses 8 and 9 list some reasons to sing thanks to God. They are general in nature and remind us that we don't have to look far to find a reason to thank God.

9. Read Psalm 147:8 and 9. What has God done for all people generally that should cause you to sing a song of thanks to Him?

10. What has God done for you specifically that should cause you to sing a song of thanks to Him?

God's Impartiality

Imagine if God played favorites based on how strong or fast or tall a person is. What a sad state a weak, slow, short person would be in. God doesn't care much about how strong a person's horse is or how powerful a person's legs are (v. 10). God delights in those who "fear him" and "hope in his mercy" (v. 11). To fear God is to believe that God is all that He says He is. Those who fear God are awed by God and don't waste their time and energy trying to awe God with who they are. Those who fear God understand that they deserve nothing but wrath from God. They learn to hope in God's merciful kindness.

What should the truths of verses 10 and 11 cause us to do? Praise the Lord! We don't serve a God Who shows favorites. Every single person—regardless of abilities or accomplishments—who fears God and hopes in His mercy will bring satisfaction to Him.

God's Work

The psalmist again interrupted his list of reasons to praise God. He gave a command. This time he turned his attention directly to Jerusalem (v. 12).

11. Read Psalm 147:13 and 14. What did God do for Jerusalem that was worthy of praise?

The book of Nehemiah records the resetting of the gates and the rebuilding of the walls in Jerusalem. Both of these jobs took a great deal of manpower.

12. Read Nehemiah 6:16. What did Israel's enemies realize when the walls and gates of Jerusalem had finally been rebuilt?

The workers who tirelessly rebuilt the walls and gates of Jerusalem poured their lives into their work, but it was God Who received the recognition and praise for the completion of the job. On the surface that scenario might seem unfair. But when we realize that nobody does anything worth noting apart from God's guiding and enabling hand, then giving God the praise for work done by mankind makes perfect sense.

God's Words

The last section of Psalm 147 deals with the praiseworthiness of God's words. When God gives a command, it happens immediately. There is no delay. Jesus' words while He was on earth demonstrated the immediate nature of God's words.

13. Read Matthew 8:3. Suppose Jesus had told the leper, "You should start to see some improvements in your leprosy in a few months. If not, I'll try again." How do you think the leper would have felt with such an unsure promise?

Some of God's commands have to do with the processes of nature. We get so accustomed to a godless explanation of the weather that we forget that nothing happens without God's directives. It is easy for us to complain as if the meteorologist were responsible for a particularly hot day or a rained-out picnic.

14. Read Psalm 147:16–18. What aspects of nature did the psalmist relegate to God's control?

15. What in nature has caused you to turn to God in praise?

God's Word

The psalmist returned to the focus on Israel in the last two verses of the psalm. The Old Testament was mainly written to or about "Jacob," a reference to the nation of Israel. God gave the Israelites all His "statutes and his judgments" (v. 19). Israel was extremely blessed to be chosen by God to receive His Word. No other nation could claim such a privilege (v. 20).

Praise the Lord that God chose to give us His Word. Without God's revelation of Himself to mankind, we would be confused and on our way to eternal separation from God. Psalm 119 is almost entirely devoted to the praise of God's Word.

16. Read the following verses in Psalm 119 and record the benefits of God's Word listed in each of the verses.

Verse 11

Verse 28

Verse 50

Verse 72

Verse 99

Verse 105

Making It Personal

17. Read Psalm 147 again as a prayer of praise to God.

18. Think of a song that picks up on one of the themes in Psalm 147. Record a few lines of the song you chose. Then sing the song as praise to the Lord.

19. Before your next worship service, prepare your heart to praise the Lord in song. Pay attention to the words and sing them as if you are personally standing before God without anyone else around.

20. Memorize Psalm 147:1.